"The Greatest Human Discovery Of All-Time!"

Breakthroughs In Both Fields of Consciousness & Astrology

By

Mark Kincaid

IN PRAISE OF THIS NEW ASTROLOGY

From Dave - US "Dear Mark, I recently received your Saturn remedies and I have to tell you right away, with just the simplest of applications, I have experienced much Saturn improvement."

From Mariola – Europe: "Thank you for your insights. Your explanations make it easier to understand what is happening every day. I am learning now how to go more with the flow and am more ready for each day, not taking things so personally. I like to analyze and see people's reactions to things, and now I'm more understanding of people's behavior and the overall events that are happening around me."

From Isabella – Spain: "Mark, thank you so very much. I used to struggle very intensely with my own, personal Saturn nature. Now, with these clearer ideas I have a wonderful checklist with which to progress better!"

From Jules – US: "Mark, I'm so thankful to have learned my chart with you recently, and those of my children. It was so wonderful this week, especially, as it was such a good opportunity to feel and observe the malefic nature of the positioning of planets and so easily understand what was happening. Knowing my children's charts also gave me greater insight into what their needs and tendencies would be. I could see what was happening and knew what was needed. It was like having a handbook for our lives and we weathered the "storm" very well this week."

From Linda – US: "Mark, your descriptions of these Transits move me in such a profound way. I have no words to express my feelings. You, Mark, are also remarkable. Thanks to you, I have found I am moving upward and am learning what causes me to "tick". One of the best things I have ever done for myself was to have a chart done by you, and to have a reading. Upon reflection, I am simply amazed regarding how you seemed to know my personality so well without ever having spoken to me prior to the reading. Again, thanks!!"

From Maria – South America: "Mark, Thank you for all your wonderful insights. I am very new to the subject although I have to say, already I feel more connected to the planets and their movements. It's lovely how you explain their movements and significance in such a clear and easy to understand way."

From Thomas – US: "I'd been deeply confused why sometimes I'd still experience negativity even after years of meditating. And, what you told me about my own personal Saturn really helped me a lot. Thank you."

From Julie – US: "Mark, I appreciate what you say. Now, I get it. All the while I've been blaming my scattered unsettledness on ADD. Learning how to be more in-tune with my Saturn has really helped me."

From Michael – US: "I LOVE YOUR WORK and love everything that you are doing."

From Susan – US: "Today my son told me that he has had his chart done by a lot of people, and that of all the people he now sees your reading as one of the most accurate. He said you really do know about a person's tendencies and inclinations. I agreed, of course."

From Uriel – US – "Mark, I just love how you write. It is accurate, precise and yet very intuitive at the same time. It also is inviting to everyone to feel out these trends for themselves while becoming aware of these general trends. I really enjoy it.

From Alice – US – "Mark, I really appreciate knowing about the transits and what effects to expect... For example, I don't wake up each morning grumbling about the abnormal cold, I'm already aware that it's a stronger possibility due to your information on this Saturn Winter. I'm more able to observe, or witness, the phenomenon without attachment."

DEDICATION

To His Holiness, Maharishi Mahesh Yogi…

Who gave me the supreme gift of meditation, which allowed
me to develop my cosmic awareness, and who inspired me to
think about astrology in a more enlightened way.
It was through his supreme guidance and knowledge
That helped me understand Saturn 'rest' better
And the great importance
Of developing our inner Saturn resources.

ISBN-13:
978-1530334391
ISBN-10:
153033439X

ACKNOWLEDGEMENTS

I'd like to first thank my parents for trying to get me to go to bed earlier and teach me about the all-important role and importance of rest in life.

I'd also like to thank my first astrology teachers who in the mid-1960's first taught me about the nature and significance of the planets of astrology.

I'd like to thank too, my eastern astrology teachers who taught me about my more accurate personal astrological chart. And, though my Saturn planet went from being Exalted in my western chart, to being much less positive in my eastern chart, still this greater self-appreciation helped me immensely in my life.

I am the most beholden to my greatest Guru, His Holiness Maharishi Mahesh Yogi who taught me the most exciting and profound of 'new', easy and effortless techniques of consciousness expansion which he simply called the unique, Transcendental Meditation technique.

I am also just as appreciative to the Maharishi for his unique insights and revelations pertaining to astrology, itself. His most extraordinary insights into astrology, as expressed in his most profound of ideas: "Astrology is For Enlightenment" are also beginning to just as profoundly change this entire field of astrology today.

I am also the most beholden to almighty God who created this supreme knowledge and wisdom of Astrology in the first place! He is after all the 'real' author and creator of this new astrology that is coming into the world today. And when you learn how to 'hear' this uniquely nature's astrology speaking to you, you will then discover that we are all, after all such "astrological beings living in just such an astrological universe!'

8

"The Greatest Human Discovery Of All-Time....!

Table of CONTENTS

INTRODUCTION

"And God said, "Let there be light," and there was light."

~ Bible – Genesis 1:3

If you had asked me what I considered to be the greatest human discovery of all-time; I might have included the invention of the wheel, or the printing press or even the creation of science!

The very moment when our entire world began to move from a pre-science culture to a past-science society – our world began changing and improving in more powerful and important ways. Because for the first time, we stopped passing on knowledge and wisdom to our children and future generations through belief and tradition. And now instead, started passing on such new knowledge and wisdom – based on the vigorous scientific process!

And who can forget of course that greatest of all scientific discoveries of all-time which was that most unusual and most creative "Einstein's – Theory of Relativity – breakthrough!

This one singular scientific breakthrough did more for science but also our world because such a pleasant personality and individual in the essential guru of Einstein made everyone feel a little bit happier about more deeply embracing this entire process of science….

Which before Einstein was perceived too often as being cold, aloof and lacking in humanity. But, Einstein was a very spiritual person, he was very compassionate and cared for our world and was therefore a great humanitarian – in addition to being a brilliant scientist.

For me, Einstein was indeed one of my greatest of natural heroes growing up and reading about him and opening myself up to how he thought – did more for me than any other teacher or guru – I could remember.

This then led me to what I now believe are the two aspects of the Greatest Human Discovery Of All-time…. which is the inherent unfoldment of our full, human potential!

Because what is it that has been the most lacking in our world, until now?

Is it more wealth, more land, more worldly or career-success?

No! The real greatest need has been for more inherent knowledge and wisdom of our inner selves….of our inner, latent potential.

I, myself, first heard of this when I was but in college and one of our psychology professors arrived one day and said to us: "Did you know you're only using 5-10% of your full potential, right now!"

Since, the year now was 1971 – very few of us had even heard this idea of human or latent potential. Today, on the other hand, this very same idea,…is everywhere!

Why even the last 4 movies I enjoyed, each of these referred to this very possibility. One of my favorites of these was that most recent Nicholas Cage movie which was called: "The Sorcerer's Apprentice." Cage of course, plays the part of the Sorcerer who then early in the movie says to his apprentice: "You have no idea what a vast and limitless potential you have."

Of course he didn't just leave with simply this idea. Most of the rest of the movie then involved the Sorcerer literally guiding and instructing his apprentice pupil in discovering for himself that he had such a profound inner potential!

Then who could forget that other most recent, "human potential movie" which is that most strange, movie "Lucy" in which Scarlett Johansson whose name is Lucy literally finds herself stumbling into her Full Human Potential within a week. Morgan Freeman is also in this movie and he serves a great role in intellectually speculating to his class of students this whole idea as to what such an increasing human potential might be like.

Then, Lucy whose found herself being catapulted into not only 5-10% but then quickly into 20, then 30, then 40, than 50 and before we know it the full 100% of her human potential! I've never seen such a movie which didn't make this whole idea of emerging human potential more attractive and palatable!

For us however, 45 years ago, way back in 1971 – we had never even heard of such a human possibility. One lone, brave student then raised their hand and asked: "Does at least modern psychology – know of any ways that we can be unfolding more and more of our latent potential?"

Suddenly, our professor looked all dismayed like the wind had just as suddenly vanished from his sails. After a long pause, he then said…."Eh,….no,…..I'm afraid…..we do not…." Then after another equally long pause of dead silence pervading the room….he seemed to get his second wind and then retorted by saying: "But, we do think that some such individuals like Albert Einstein for example, might have been using as much as 15% of his latent potential."

I didn't feel better in hearing this. I actually felt worse. Because if our greatest scientist of all-time was only using 15% of his potential – what possible hope could there be for the rest of us.

After these lectures I found myself wandering around on our college campus and wondering what I was even doing in school, when I'd now become aware of the greatest need in of human life! I now believed that I knew what my greatest need was on the other hand this very same educational science of psychology had also told me that such traditional venues or institutions are relatively helpless in terms of helping us find the answer to this greatest human need.

I found myself adrift, rambling around on campus, looking for something I knew not. Though, it is said sometimes: "That when God closes a door, he also opens a window somewhere else." One day then as was wandering about, my eyes spied this very unusual looking poster on one of our college, student union kiosks that held a picture of a very strange looking man and the title at the top simply said:

"Learn Transcendental Meditation & Unfold Your Full Human Potential!"

I thought it was a joke. Perhaps some of my college friends were punking me and lurking around about to spring forth and say, trick or treat! Then I had a vision of that famous TV host, Alan Funt, lurking in the bushes somewhere and he then burst out to say: "Surprise! You're on Candid Camera!"

I waited for a moment to see if either of these possibilities were going to manifest now and when neither one did, I thought: "Perhaps I'm in one of those kinds of déjà vu or serendipitous moments that you sometimes hear about."

Fortunately, I also had a college friend, named Roger who'd been trying to drag me to one such Transcendental Meditation introductory lecture. For some reason I'd been resisting him. Then that one day I told him about our recent psychology classes and that T.M. poster on campus so I said to him: "So, do the T.M. people really believe we can now unfold our full potential!

He just smiled the most strange and peculiar, Cheshire cat smile and then said: "Absolutely!" Well, I couldn't possibly believe it was true. Though the coincidence of our most recent psychology classes couldn't be denied. I knew I had to go to my introductory T.M. lecture just in case it was true. I attended that lecture and remember thinking to myself: "Even if only 10% of these most outrageous benefits that our lecturer talked about – could come true for me, that alone would be enough of a reason for me to at least try."

I even went up afterward and told our lecturer about our most recent psychology classes and then I asked him: "So, do you really mean that we can now be unfolding our full, human potential?" He smiled again, that most nauseating, ear to ear grin, like he too had the greatest secret inside of himself and he then said: "Yes, yes…! See, Albert Einstein might have used as much as 15% of his human potential but he was after all, only a master of the relative. Because when you learn to meditate you will become a master of the absolute!"

I of course had no idea what he was talking about. But, I now knew that I was at least going to look into this, even if some small portion of it could be true. A week later then found me driving my yellow, graveyard shift taxi up to the door of our college town's Ramada Inn where I then received my first ever, unfoldment of human potential – mantra!

I was not disappointed a bit.

In fact, even in that very first 20-minute meditation my whole heart and mind, my very soul, soared to such new heights than I would have ever thought possible!

And while I was in the deepest kind of interior reverie – I heard this very far off little voice beckoning me back home, innocently saying to me: "Was it easy….?"

I laughed because it had been in fact the most easy thing I had ever done.

I was now in some kind of great, cosmic, delightful shock.

Every day that I was now meditating, I really did begin feeling that more and more of my interior – something was indeed, now unfolding for me.

After six months I had one of the most surprising and yet, clear examples of my greater interior potential unfolding. It was in-between semesters and I was at the registrar's office to sign up for my next crop of courses. After picking those classes that I needed for my major I then had a chance to pick a few electives. I first picked an art class – I always wished that I had been more artistic in my life.

Secondly, I found myself seriously considering taking a public speaking class. Though, my inner voiced railed back at me, saying: "Are you crazy! You know how much you dislike speaking in public?" I couldn't believe I was even seriously thinking of taking such a class. Though, something inside of me, made me do this. Another week later then found me sitting in my first Public Speaking class and again, lamenting the fact that I was now consciously choosing to add such stress into my life. I was even panicking a bit, feeling stressed and about to spring into flight running away from my present stressor.

But, before I could leap back through the door, our professor arrived and then bellowed for all to hear: "Okay, everyone who'd like to be first? Please stand up and tell us about yourself!" Of course no one moved, we all seemed to feel trapped in that very same kind of stressful situation. He then continued saying: "Come on people, this is after all, a public speaking class."

Again, a deadly silence was sitting there immobilizing all of us. Suddenly, one brave soul raised their hand and now I could relax. But, then it hit me: "Wait! Wait…that's my hand,…quick Mark, lower it ….perhaps I can pretend to have been stretching." Our professor, however, was not fooled. He then said: Very good, please stand up and introduce yourself and tell us a little bit about yourself."

Well, by now I was feeling dizzy as I tried to stand I'm sure I was swaying back and forth. The palms of my hands were so sweating and my mouth and lips were parched. What I really needed was a glass of water but I was committed. I stood and attempted to speak, most of the time, my eyes downward, lest I catch the very depressing grins of others laughing at my demise.

I plopped back down after some of the longest 2-minutes I could ever remember and then continued to kick my inner self for making a choice to put myself into such a familiar, though stressful situation. That night too I reflected on 'why' and even why I had chosen to be first. At least when I was younger I could put off speaking as long as possible. And sometimes, that persistent resistance allowed me to not be called on at all!

Tonight however, a different thought occurred to me: "You know it was quite brilliant to be first. Because in being first, you got it over with, right away and you didn't have to sit there during that whole hour, worrying and anxious that your time would be next!"

I also wondered why I had chosen to be first and then even, why I had consciously chosen to take this stupid course, in the first place. Then it hit me:

"I think it's because I've been now meditating for a short, six months. I mean, right away, I've been feeling more strong and powerful within myself. And, now, I even could find the internal fortitude to try and get over one of my most stressful of all life-experiences – which has been this intense fear of speaking in front of others!"

Then I realized just how cool this was because I hadn't been taking any classes on getting over my fear of speaking. I'd not even been reading any books nor practicing any kinds of life-affirmations. I'd simply been meditating and each day, feeling stronger and stronger from within!

I then began to think too: "So, this is what a smidgen of such greater human potential, unfolding, ...feels like."

Within a year I remember then having the most surprising of all such experiences. I experienced almighty God for the very first time!

Though again, I wasn't trying to. I wasn't reading any such books on how to find God. I wasn't trying to culture more receptivity, more openness or make myself more worthy. I was simply meditating each day and only 20 minutes twice a day, brought me this greatest of all, life-experiences.

I was still in school and going to my first class, one fine morning. Though, I was early for a change and had a few moments before my first class. So, I lay down for a moment to catch a few winks and before I knew it, I was fast asleep. Then, almost just as quickly,…..I found myself….as if,….waking up from such an intense, vivid dream!

I'd just dreamt of my mother from Chicago. And I felt sooo elated. She was seated on a coach and I, at her feet was sitting on a kind of rug while she lightly stroked my hair and hear. She also conveyed to me without speaking this most soothing of thoughts: "Everything will be okay….."

And I awoke, more elated and more illuminated than I could ever remember. Then I began to think: "But, you know, she didn't look like my mother in Chicago!" And though, I knew you didn't always have to dream of exactly who you were dreaming about, whilst dreaming…..

It then hit me: "She wasn't my mother from Chicago,…she was in fact,….my,…eh,….." And here I didn't even have a word for it, so I eventually said: "She's….my eh,…God….Mother!"

And I now 'knew' in my deepest of heart that I had just had my very first direct experience of almighty God! From this very moment I know knew that God existed and the strangest of all such God-revelations was that "He"….was also a divine, "She!"

It would be a few years before I'd come across another kind of Maharishi Mahesh Yogi lecture where he would just innocently mention that: "When you start to experience God – the form that is the most pleasing to you,…will be the one ….that comes to you!

I couldn't believe it. I'd never even heard of God as Mother. Growing up in the west, in my Christian background, I always just assumed that God was male, God the Father you know. So, it was of course so very fulfilling to find that He was also a She!

I then thought again,…."So, this is what more and more

unfolding human potential feels like!" I of course kept meditating because this was, without a doubt the greatest, single opportunity that I found myself stumbling into, over my entire life!

Six years later then passed and I found myself aware of that most intriguing eastern system of astrology for the first time. I'd of course, grown up only knowing about western astrology which I had studied years earlier in my late teens and early adult hold, also while being in college. And because I'd had such an initially positive western astrology experience and now so many wonderful years of such positive experiences within such diverse eastern philosophies as meditating, yoga and even something called Ayurveda; I found myself particularly intrigued to now look into eastern astrology.

The very first thing I noticed was just how similar this system was to western astrology. This eastern, Jyotish or Vedic astrology also believe in the very same kind of premise that: "The star and planets from above, on the days of our births, will describe who we will be and even why we will get born with the unique personalities and human strengths and weaknesses that we will be found, living."

I then discovered too how this system also believed in the very same structure of the so-called "astrological chart" which represents a unique kind of snap-shot of that actual sky when we were born. I even now discovered how this system too believed in many of the same kinds of meaning and even significance of the basics of astrology which are called one's Planets, Signs and Houses of one's individual astrology chart!

I now found one particular aspect to this new to me, eastern astrology which was so very different than my western chart.

There was a whopping 23-degree difference between both of these two, systems. This meant that all of one's western planets would now be found 'backward', these very same, 23-degrees!

And because there are only 30 such degrees in each of these 12 Signs of astrology I then realized that many people's new eastern planets will be found in completely different Signs! For me, personally, not only did all of my planets go backward, these same, 23-degrees. But for me, all of my western planets now moved into literally different, previous Signs!

My western Sun which had been in the #6 Sign of Virgo, now suddenly went backward into that previous, #5 Sign of Leo. And my personal Moon planet which had been in that #7 Sign of Libra, according to my western chart; now moved backward, into that previous #6 Sign of Virgo according to my new, eastern chart.

Initially, I couldn't even imagine how such a different, eastern chart could also fit me since so much of my previous western chart, already had. However, I was still sufficiently intrigued enough to at least look into this new, most attractive, deep and complicated eastern, Vedic astrology so I picked up a few eastern books and then eventually, found myself studying this new system in much the same way I'd previously studied my western chart.

In the 1960's and 70's, there were all kinds of Sun-Signs books and books that had such natural descriptions as to just what it was supposed to be like to have one's very planets within the unique Signs of one's chart. So, when I found that my Sun was supposed to be in that #6 Sign of Virgo – I then went to that chapter on Virgo. I did the same thing for my Moon planet in #7 Libra and my Mars planet, in that very different, #5 Sign of Leo.

I now did the same thing for my new, so very different eastern chart. Though instead of reading about my Sun, supposedly being in that #6 Sign of Leo, I read about what it was supposed to be like, if found in that so very different and previous, #5 Sign of Leo.

I then discovered just how much more accurately and profoundly my new eastern chart fit me; which of course quite shocked me since so much of my previous western chart, already had. I wondered now why I had related so much to my western chart, especially since my so very different eastern chart, also fit me, so very profoundly!

I then realized – In those areas of my western chart that I had related to the most; my Virgo, Libra and Leo planets, I still had such Virgo, Libra and Leo planets according to my new, eastern chart, though the exact planetary reasons for these were now, so very different.

Now, however, as I learned more and more about each of these most significant details of my new, eastern chart, I quickly realized that literally, 100% of my eastern chart, profoundly fit me! Whereas now, I realized that in truth, only about 30% of my previous western chart, actually had.

In such future chapters in this 1st Section of our book here, we'll go into such greater detail so you too can see just how much more accurately your own, personal eastern chart can be, for you.

Next, I encountered one surprising aspect of my new eastern chart which I didn't like. There was such a very surprising and kind of mysterious, "fatalism" existing within all of the present, eastern astrology books that I'd been studying. This was the very distinct feeling that one's chart is in fact, "written in stone" and is therefore incapable of being either changed or improved!

This was of course quite disappointing to me because being from the west, especially the U.S. where even the very constitution here says: "Anyone can grow up to be President" This means then such a different belief and mind-set that one can instead, grow and self-improve within one's life and even become that much more successful and fulfilled. This of course was a far cry from that very fatalism which was more like predetermined, destiny being inevitable for one. I then found myself drifting away from even this much more accurate and precisely profound, eastern astrology because I couldn't find any way to look past that intense fatalism that was even quite depressive to read about.

From here I pretty much stopped thinking about astrology. I did, however, have that most wondrous, unfolding of our full potential, consciousness expansion techniques and even such technologies to continue exploring and growing with.

In fact, I thought I was pretty much done with astrology, so 10 years later when I ended up finding myself in India – I was quite surprised to find myself aware of such a Vedic astrology again. Though, this time I got introduced to a very different and unusual, Maharishi vision of astrology. For the Maharishi, the chief architect of this most surprising and monumental of consciousness expansion breakthroughs which he simply called Transcendental Meditation – he also had something very unique and surprising to say about astrology.

Though, for the first 25 days of our 30-day stay there in India, we were attending to, such 25 days of such wonderful and profound Ayurvedic lectures. I was but one of over 450 other individuals from all over the world and we all were listening to some of the most brilliant Ayurvedic minds, teachers, physicians and even gurus of Ayurveda for our first 25 days!

Then, the Maharishi then came to us on this 25th day and said to our course liaison, a German physician; "Uli, do they know Jyotish?" Uli then said: "Eh,….no Maharishi…we didn't think to add such a segment…." The Maharishi continued, saying: "No, they must know Jyotish. Jyotish and Ayurveda go together."

We then had such a fast and furious Jyotish course which became for many people, one of their favorite parts of our course there. Though, they couldn't find any formal Indian, professional astrologers or Jyotishees as they are called, to teach us. Instead they ended up settling on a fellow course participant who was in fact, a professional western astrologer who just happened to know enough Jyotish to teach us. We heard from him, during the day-time hours about the basics of astrology which included these Planets, Sign and Houses.

Most of these lectures where pretty familiar to me since I'd already studied both of these two, traditional western and eastern astrology systems. However, nothing I'd ever read, in fact, nothing I'd ever even heard of; prepared me for what came to us in our evening hours.

For these last five, evening days of our course – we heard from the Maharishi himself about his unique "vision of astrology". For the Maharishi, "astrology is all about enlightenment!"

I was in pleasant shock. Because nowhere in all of such traditional astrology's had there ever been such a novel or most unique of profound ideas of astrology and enlightenment together. These last five-days of our course flew by and before I realized, I was back in the states here. Though, I'd gone to India, originally to attend this 30-day course in Ayurveda and receive such new training and credentials to then take such a natural healing system of Ayurveda to the many doctors and physician's offices in my home town. Now, instead I found myself thinking of astrology again.

But, now wondering: "What had I missed before, in all of my previous astrological study?" So, I pulled out all of my many, western and eastern astrology books and wondered what had been missing in all of these such that this most important and most profound idea of "astrology and enlightenment" had been for so very long, missing in such traditional astrology systems.

It took me about a year but in about 12 months – I finally began to sense what I had missed and what had long been missing. I then realized that what had been most absent, was such a clear understanding as to the inherent "Self-development" nature and potential of astrology. Previously, what has long been dominant is what we could call the natural "diagnostic" aspect of astrology. This consists of trying to help people to discover, just 'how' their personal charts, really do fit them. But, very little has been known or practiced in terms of just 'how'…we're meant to be able to grow and most profoundly self-improve within ourselves ….from this very same astrology.

I then began wondering if such a greater planetary self-growth was indeed possible and I then had one of the greatest astrological revelations of my entire life! I realized that many of my especially, most negative and undeveloped, birth planets, like my Moon and Saturn planets; had actually grown most profoundly from simply meditating and practicing other such Maharishi – enlivened – Vedic sciences like yoga and Ayurveda!

My Moon-planet which had been so very symbolic of my many, emotional and mental problems growing up; already had grown from so many wonderful years of simply meditating. Now, I began to see too, how my inherent Saturn planet too had, vastly improved. Where previously, my Saturn appreciation of the inherent and most profound, role of rest in life – was sorely lacking due to being born with such a so-called negative Saturn planet from my birth.

Now, I began to see just how much this very different Saturn part of me had grown by simply being exposed to such Saturn wise and Saturn rich Vedic sciences like meditation, yoga and Ayurveda. Meditation, itself, profoundly enlivens the depth of Saturn silence within one. Such Yoga exercises, bending and stretching will also improve the very Saturn balanced that is necessary. And finally, especially Ayurveda was particularly most rich and profound in such Saturn-wisdom; because it taught just how one can be improving one's very Saturn-nature by simply discovering how to become more in-tune with such natural rhythms which are called the Vata, pita and Kapha cycles of life. There are such cycles of each day, such cycles of each month and even such seasonal cycles that one can discover; all of which will have the most surprising and yet profound effect of literally, enlivening one's own, very Saturn nature!

So, now I began exploring just how such an improved and more "enlightenment", self-development astrology might be found. And, I began exploring and discovering more and more such amazing and profound ways in which astrology itself could be used as such a rich and most extraordinary of self-growth tools.

Though, what started out in 1988 as a very fascinating inquiry, quickly blossomed into a full blown, self-development passion which then expanded into over 25 years of such research and discoveries of just how such an astrology can now be both understood and practiced as the most important and profound of "self-transformational" tools!

Somewhere along this long line of self-discovery I then realized that both together, this most recent consciousness breakthrough which is simply called Transcendental Meditation and now this most striking and almost unbelievable astrological breakthrough as to the very self-development nature of astrology – both together represent the single, greatest human discovery of all-time!

Because with these two, simultaneous activities – you will have found two such most important ways in which you can be unfolding your complete, human potential. And this unfoldment of our latent, 100% - human potential is by far the most important of all such human accomplishments that we could achieve in this life. These two most significant, consciousness and astrological breakthroughs together, represent the singular greatest discovery of all! In a 1st Section we will discuss each of these most important changes going on now. Then in a 2nd Section we will discuss how YOU can take such greater advantage of this greatest discovery of all…..!

Section 1

How I Stumbled – Into This Very Greatest Human Discovery Of All-Time!……..!

> "We need not feel ashamed of flirting with the zodiac. The zodiac is well worth flirting with."
>
> ~ D. H. Lawrence

I of course never knew that I was being led to the greatest human discovery of all-time. I was simply following the unique morsels of bread that I innocently found spread out before me.

However, from that very moment when I first even discovered just how much my western chart fit me – I knew that there was something to this whole 'astrology' thing which alone, quite shocked and transformed meBecause unlike most people, unlike those millions of people who don't have this greatest blessing to truly understanding 'why' – they continue struggling and suffering under this most distinct experience of confusion and a lack of such self-understanding.

In addition, most people feel that life is unjust and that there is no true reason why most things happen to people. This very chaotic way of seeing the universe then continues to contribute to this greatest ignorance which has been going on for so very long and no real solutions are found within most people's experiences. This of course then led me to meditating because nothing within the western system has been about 'how' we might be able to improve our very planets. This then led me to that much more accurate and profound eastern system of astrology where I then discovered 'exactly' what it can be like to find out how literally, 100% of one's complete eastern chart, does in fact, more precisely fit one!

Even now, over 35 years later – I look back and realize what a great milestone it was to discover so very clearly, just how significant it is to find such a unique astrological reason for everything. No wonder this so very well-developed eastern system alone has become so much more popular in our world today.

However, this extremely new, self-development breakthrough makes even that much more accurate eastern system – to be suddenly that much more understandable and profound.

Because when you too discover how your chart fits you but also how there is the most distinct and powerful technology for self-growth – there within these very same details of your chart, then you too will have this very same experience of discovering the "greatest human discovery of all-time!"

And unlike all other such great human discoveries – every time every new human individual has this very same, astrological, human self-revelation – the sense of this greatest profundity will become even more well established and significant.

For example, though it took me decades to find this greatest human discovery of all-time – in most of my most recent students – they're able to have this very same, greatest of human discoveries – in a much shorter amount of time.

Whereas it took me over 15 years to go through all of my western and eastern charts – you now can learn your own chart in several months. And whereas it took me over 25 years to discover 'how' such an astrology could be so self-development oriented; YOU now can find this same level of self-growth within even a few such short years!

28

CHAPTER 1

MY 1ST - TRADITIONAL WESTERN ASTROLOGY-SELF-AWAKENING....!

"The two most important days in your life,
are the day you were born and the day,
you find out why."

~ Mark Twain

As I now read something like this:

"Sun in Virgo individuals are analytic, cerebral, highly
intellectual oriented and many are also very self-critical and
fault finding upon others. Such Virgo's too can be very
fastidious and perfectionist oriented, as well."

I then found myself reflecting on all that I read, I then remembered many for instances and very real, practical examples and experiences in which I had been literally, very Virgo-like, over my entire life.

For example, my very first memory of Virgo came to me from a story our mother used to tell. So, if you were a friend of our family or a guest in our home or my mother simply wanted to tease me; she'd pull out this old story! Also, she told this story so often, I must have heard it 10 times growing up. And she told it so well, I thought you might enjoy hearing her telling this story, herself:

Our Mother - "Did you know that there's a controversy today between whether nurturing children or children's nature, is more important? I used to always believe that my children were a kind of blank slate and that what I could do to nourish and nurture them was vastly more important.

Then, one day I had an experience that totally changed my mind. Mark and Laura, (one of my sisters by the way.) were so very little and I wanted to put them outside to play, in our family sand-box while I did some chores in the kitchen. Since I could see them through our kitchen window I didn't worry about them.

However, a few minutes later I heard the kitchen screen door, squeaking open and there was little Mark, waddling toward me with the most distressed look on his face. His hands were all extended in the air while he kept saying, 'Dirty, dirty!' When I went to see what was the matter, I couldn't find any dirt at all. I did notice however, the moment I wiped off his little hands, that he immediately felt better. I allowed him to stay inside until it was time to go check on Laura.

And, there she was in that same ol' wonderful family sand-book. But by now, she was covered in some 'real' dirt', from head to toe! When I went to clean her up I found her reaction to be equally as strange. She simply said: 'NO, NO! I don't want to go!"

From this very moment I realized there was something very different and unique within each of my children that had nothing to do with how I raised or nurtured them."

I grew up as you might imagine, mostly hating this story. Only later would I read that many Virgo's don't like to be teased or criticized. Eventually, I came to love this story because it then become my very first example of some aspect of my personal astrology, profoundly fitting me! I also came to appreciate this story because it became my first realization that others too had their own, unique astrological natures and personalities.

For me now, I found myself living with this very new and

unique Virgo sense of myself for a number of years and also found myself living such a deeper appreciation of myself than ever before. Already some of that great confusion and frustrations began to diminish for me – with even this one singular, Sun-planetary, greater self-understanding. I also began discovering how other people too could be better understood by reflecting on their unique Sun-Sign, as well.

Then, after about two years of this – I found myself aware for the first time – that there were some such other Virgo's who didn't quite seem like me. So, even though they too were born within this same month of Virgo – as I was – I noticed that they had very different personalities than I did. So, I wondered why this was true.

Which then led me to my next astrological phase which was what can be called the "complete astrological chart." This was that one is much more than just a Sun-Sign kind of human personality. I then discovered that I was supposed to have as many as 10 such other planets in Signs – which I was instantly curious about – especially since so much of my initial western Sun-Sign descriptions had already fit me!

I then sent away for my first complete western astrological chart and six-weeks later received a 20-page computer generated description of my complete western chart. I now saw that I had many other planets in Signs descriptions. I had something called a Moon planet in the #7 Sign of Libra. I even had a Mars-planet in the very distinct #5 Sign of Leo.

Within even a couple days of reading all about my new, complete chart I found myself self-awakening to these very different and unique Virgo, Libra and Leo, qualities and characteristics that I'd long been living but rarely understanding until now.

I remembered such unique Libra times where I was in fact, the Libra peace maker in my home and with my friends. I also quite agreed with that other Libra quality which is described as an ability to hear both sides of any issue.

And for those of you who would like to follow this discussion of my western astrology journey – by following my chart – I'm including a copy of it which includes both Planets & Signs.

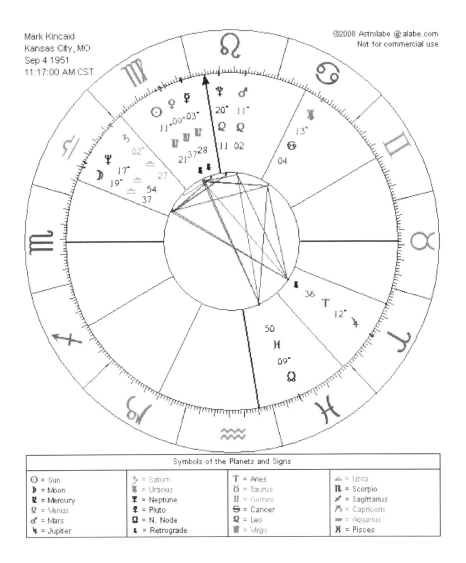

Mark Kincaid
Kansas City, MO
Sep 4 1951
11:17:00 AM CST

©2008 Astrolabe @ alabe.com
Not for commercial use

Symbols of the Planets and Signs			
☉ = Sun	♄ = Saturn	♈ = Aries	♎ = Libra
☽ = Moon	♅ = Uranus	♉ = Taurus	♏ = Scorpio
☿ = Mercury	♆ = Neptune	♊ = Gemini	♐ = Sagittarius
♀ = Venus	♇ = Pluto	♋ = Cancer	♑ = Capricorn
♂ = Mars	☊ = N. Node	♌ = Leo	♒ = Aquarius
♃ = Jupiter	℞ = Retrograde	♍ = Virgo	♓ = Pisces

These planets are depicted by those unique western symbols which you might already be familiar with. The Sun, for example is represented by the symbol of a circle or "O" with a dot in the middle.

⊙

That Sun or ⊙ part of my chart was found directly below that unique symbolism for Virgo which appears directly above it, and which looks like this: ♍ Virgo In other words, my Sun was in Virgo according to my western chart. Then I located up my personal Moon planet which was depicted in this western system as a crescent Moon shape which looked like this:

☽ ! All the other planets too are found within other unique "slices of a pie" and are also found directly below other

Sign-symbolisms. For my Moon and Saturn ♄ planets, for example, both of these are found directly below that unique

♎
Libra

symbolism for Libra which looks like this: ♎ Libra

The other chief planetary configuation I noticd was that my

unique Mars planet or ♂ was also found flowing in a very different slice of a pie and directly below another new Sign

♌

symbolism of Leo which was this unique symbol: ♌ At some point too I found a total list of all of my specific planets which then helped me begin to understand that I'd been born with a much more elaborate and complicated human nature or presonality than I ever thought, before!

My Western Planets:	Degrees & Signs
Sun	11 Degrees Virgo
Moon	19 Degrees Libra
Rising Sign	16 Degrees Scorpio
Mercury	3rd Degree Virgo
Venus	9th Degree Virgo
Mars	11th Degree Leo
Jupiter	12th Degree Aries
Saturn	2nd Degree Libra
Rahu	9th Degree Pisces
Ketu	9th Degree Virgo
Neptune	17th Degree Libra
Uranus	13th Degree Cancer
Pluto	9th Degree Pisces

I now began studying or reading about my new and unique, other planetary descriptions as I'd done with my Sun and then quickly found that I related the most to my Libra and Leo planets as well as my Virgo ones.

I encountered something like this when I found that I was supposed to have been born with my Moon within this unique #7 Sign of Libra. I read something like this: "Moon in Libra individuals love harmony! They also do not like discord and quite often will find themsleves beeing the natural peacemakers in their environments. Also, such Librans have the most unique ability to "see both sides of any issue or life-circumstance."

I then again, looked within and wondered too, whether or not these so very different Libra descriptions also fit me. I then found myself remembering other for instances and expreiences in which I had been in fact, very Libra-like, growing up. One time for example, I remembered how much I hated for there to be discord in my high-school, classes. One day, for example, I remembered how much I hated that feeling of stress right before we had to do our regular oral reports!

There was such a palatable tension in the air because so many, especially myself; were so nervous at the fact that we were going to have to stand up and make such public speaking, oral reports, disasters!

I then remembered how often I liked to make jokes to try and make everyone laugh just because I wanted to try and diminish that so very intense tension that was happpening during these times. I now discovred why I did this. It was because of this Libra part of me that it even occurred to me to try and get rid of this unharmonious tension that was going on.

I also remembered too that I had that other distinct Libra quality of naturally seing the other 'side'. I noticd this manifesting quite often whenever there would be political discussions being expressed. I more often than not, identified with being a kind of liberal type of person. But, in spite of this, even if I'd hear some people spouting out such uniquely "liberal" points of view; I would find myself often both thinking about and then expressing the completely opposite, even "conservative" point of view!

This naturally surprised me and I never understood why I did this or had this kind of aspect to my natural, human personality until I found myself reading about Libra planets.

I then found myself reading about my Mars planet being in that unique #5 Sign of Leo which was also supposed to be highly indicative of another aspect to my human personality. When I read about Mars being in Leo, I read something like this: "Mars in Leo individuals are very regal and kingly like. They quite often find themselves with a lot of self-confidence and self-worth. And, many such Leo's will love their independence and often too will find themselves having businesses of their own."

I also found myself quite vividly relating to most of these new, Leo, descriptions and I especially related to that unique quality of regalness. Ever since I was a kid I remember feeling like a little prince! I also related the most vividly to that Biblical storiy of the prodigal son. He was the young son of a wealthy merchant who'd gone away from home to seek his own fortune. I realized in this story how much I had felt like I too was one such, most deserving of individuals and quite vividly felt like too was one of God's, special children!

In fact, quite often I would also wonder why I'd been born in such a poor family in the first place. I even asked my dad one time: "How come we don't have more money!" My dad laughed and then said: "It's because I had six children!"

I also related to those many other unique Leo ideas like loving being one's own boss and independence. I remembered too the very first business of my own that I had, when I was also in high school. And, though it was just a simple lawn mowing business, I realized now how much I had loved pushing around my little lawn more quite often working some very long hours for myslf! My dad too was surprised about this because so often I was so glued to the TV, I think he was afraid I'd grow up lazy.

I also read about the so-called negative side of Leo, at this time as well. Every Sign by the way has both a positive and negative side. Leo's chief negatives include being more selfish, self-centered and self-absorbed in one's life. I then remembered my very first memory of being eh, more selfish which occurred on one such, glorious Christmas day, morning!

We had just finishd devouring all of our Christmas presents and I then looked up to our mother and said in such a frenzy:

"Is that all I get!" I then watched as her sweet face completely dropped and she was suddenly so saddened and disappointed that I could say such a selfish thing. For years, I dismissed this as being due to being a more selfish, young kind of person. Later, however when I began to better understand myself especially from this Leo point of view, I realized I "was more selfish" than I previously understood.

I also read such other Mars in Leo qualities as these: "Many Mars in Leo individuals will choose to be in the military or police forces and quite often feel that they want to be the policemen in their environments. They also will tend to be more intense in these Leo qualities just because their Mars-nature is in this unique Sign."

At this time, I found that I didn't quite relate so clearly to this other, Mars description though it would be years before I'd hear about the eastern chart and how my Marish-self had moved into that very #4 Sign of Cancer!

I next found myself reading about something called the Moon's "Size" which is so very different than all of the planet's "Signs". The idea here was that the literal Size of sunlight that will be found shining upon one's Moon, planet will then describe how strong or weak one will be emotinoally. For example, those born under very big and bright, waxing Moon's will be those kinds of persons who will be born with a very steady and strong, even mature Moon or emotional part of themselves.

Those on the other hand who get born under very dim or dark, small or waning Moons, will be those kinds of individuals who will get born with many kinds of emotional and mental challenges, in their lives. And since I'd long experienced myself as being a very shy, self-conscious and especially depressive kind of personality, I found this one, unique aspect of my more complete western chart, to be the most revealing and right on, for me personally.

Instinctivly I began looking for any ways in which I might be able to improve this important Moon part of myself. Unfortunately there were no such ideas in traditonal astrology.

And though a number of these unique aspects of my western chart had also fit me, there was almost no emphasis on what one might be able to do to improve oneself through improving or strengenting one's especially most negative of planets.

I did however, relish this greater clarity about mysef and I felt much understood and clear as to who I was.

I didn't of course know 'whom' I was supposed to evolve into.

Butl, this sense that I now knew myself more clearly, was itself quite wonderful and surprsing.

Though, now I knew why so many people made such a fuss about this whole astrology thing.

And I couldn't figure out why so many disliked astrology so much. Because I'd now experienced so very clearly how so many importgant aspects of my new western chart did in fact profoundly fit me!

Though, at this stage I hadn't ever heard of that new western system of Sidereal astrology which had only recently been created about twenty-five years earlier by Cyril Fagan. Though, to be fair, very few westenr astrology students had ever heard of this new, western breakthrough which he now was calling western Sidereal astrology.

And I'd never yet been exposed to that more accurate eastern

—

astrology, nor either of these two fatalisitc or enlightenment perspectives.

I had however, now been exposed to one of the most significant things you can experinece in this life; which is 'where' within yourself you are the most underdevelped and the most negative or dysfunctional.

My new western chart had at least made me so much more aware of just how my personal Moon-nature was so very represnetative of such an important part of my inner life that could benefit from improving!

And though very little within this traditional western astology was able to help me to discover 'how' I might be improving and growing within my very real, inteiror Moon-mental side.

Still, at least now I was looking.

I had no idea where it might lead me, though I found it helpful to at least know now, that I might be able to benefit if I could discover how to grow and self-improve within this all-important Moon-part of my inner life.

Fortunatley, almighty God might have had this same idea in mind.

Because on most college campuses at this time there were all kinds of many, meditaiton and yoga practices which I would soon discover, could in fact, have the most immediate and profound improvement on my very Moon – emotional and mental side of myself!

I also found myself much more self-seen as I'd now discovered three such unique Virgo, Libra and Leo – aspects to that very unique astrological personality that I'd long been living but rarely understanding until now!

So, if you've never read about your 'complete' astrological chart and only now about your so-called Sun-Sign – than you are really only understanding about 10% of your real, complete astrological nature.

There are also such unique 'books' within this unqiue western astrological system which in retrospect – gave me the greatest ability to discover my own, astrological nature, by myself.

These were the so-called "Looking up one's own chart" books. These are whole books that have whole chapters on what the planets will be like when found within the unique Signs that we were born with.

When I read about these – I found myelf the most self-awakening to that very real and distinct human, astrological personality I had long been living but rarely truly understanding until now.

Though, this western astrology experience – wouldn't be the end for me and very soon – I'd even find a much more accurate, 23-degree different eastern system of astrology for myself.

However, from this very moment I knew that there was something very real and significant to this very astrological thing – and just how so much of my very real and distinct human personality – could be so very better understood – by looking at myself through this unique lens or mirror of this very astrology. And so will you too, have such an important and profound, greater Self-awakening. Because as it turns out, each one of us, are already such unique "astrological beings – living in such a unique astrological universe and the sooner we each, realize this – the better off we will be!

CHAPTER 2

MY PERSONAL EXPERIENCE OF THIS CONSCIOUSNESS-BREAKTHROUGH....!

"The key to growth is the introduction of higheri dimensions of consciousness into our awareness."

~ Lao Tzu

Unfortunately, there were not so many ways or suggestions coming from this traditional western system of astrology as to 'how' I might be able to improve my interior Moon-nature. So I found myself looking elsewhere. Fortunately, the year now was 1971 and on most college campuses there were all kinds of almost innumerable meditation and yoga techniques available. I also had a college friend named Roger who'd been trying to take me to one such, Transcendental Meditation, introductory lecture. For some reason, I'd been resisting going.

Perhaps the idea of sitting around and contemplating my navel, didn't seem to have much of an allure for me. However, the very moment that I then later heard that Transcendental Meditation could also dramatically improve one's very mind, suddenly I found myself more eager to hearing about meditating.

I then went to my first introductory T.M. lecture and felt like "Even if only 10% of the benefits that were being described here, could come true for me; that alone would be enough of a reason for me to at least try to meditate!"

A week later found me driving my yellow, graveyard shift taxi up to the door of our college town's Ramada Inn where I then received my first ever, Moon strengthening mantra!

I was not disappointed.

In fact even from that very first, 20-minute meditation I noticed feeling immediately more emotionally, calm and settled than ever, before! Of course I kept meditating and after even one single month, noticed that I felt more Moon, quiet, still and at peace than my entire life.

I was naturally, very taken by this huge, consciousness opportunity of meditating and what later I would hear described as "consciousness expansion". I found myself dramatically shifting into this unique human potential improvement that is only possible when one learns how to literally expand one's mind and interior consciousness through meditating.

I also began realizing at this point that many of the so-called negative, planetary aspects to my personality began to become less negative. My many, more emotionally charged Moon negatives became right away less negative. Where I had so often felt so much worrying, anxieties and even depression in my life now, suddenly, that all of that began to disappear!

Even my intuition began to improve which quite surprised me since I'd never been intuitive, before.

I noticed too how my Leo, selfishness seemed to be shifting, too. Whereas before I'd often felt so much more concerned about myself, now as I began to feel 'fuller' within and also noticed feeling more giving and self-less! This was especially surpising since the T.M. experience included no trying to change or other such life-affirmations. One simply meditated and immediately felt more whole from within oneself. I was also now exploring what later would turn out to be the literal 'best' of all such even, astrological human self-development tools.

Because as it turns out, its not enough that we just discover 'how' our charts fit us. But, it is even more important that we then discover 'how'....we can be improving and self-developing ourselves.

These new, many Vedic science experiences I was now having from both meditating and other such disciples as yoga and even something called Ayurveda – which is the natuarl health system of Vedic science – all of these began to help me to see that I could be most dramatically and most profoundly, self-growing within myself.

These many new so-called eastern philosophies experiences – would also end up leading me to my first exposure to that eastern astrological system – which would then have an even more powerful experience in my present astrological journey.

Perhaps because I'd already had so many positive, previous westenr astrology experiences and also now, so many positive eastern disciples – experiences – but I found myself particularly intrigued to look into my new, eastern chart.

Right away I found this new eastern system to be very similar to westenr astrology. It also believed in that very same, basic premise which is that "The stars and planets on the day of one's birth – will in fact, most profoundly fit one!"

I then discovered how this system too believed in the same idea of the astrological chart – which is a kind of snapshot of that actual sky on that day in which we were born.

This system too believed in the very same structure of the astrological chart – including the three basic components of these same astrological charts – which are called the Planets,

Signs and Houses of astrology.

I next discovered how this system too – also believed in many of the same kinds of meanings of these very same planets, Signs and Houses.

The planets of astrology for example represent the essential details of what it means to be such a natural human being. Everyone has one such Sun-nature within them which corresponds quite exactly – to that exact, I, ego and self-nature that one has always been.

Such astrology's also describe how the unique Signs that one's planets are in – then will describe more about that unique human personality and human strengths and weaknesses one got born with.

Though, fairly quickly I then discovered the chief difference between one's western and eastern charts.

There is a whopping 23-degree difference between one's westenr and eastern chats which means all of one's 'western' planets will now be found, backward, these same, exact, 23-degrees. And because there are only 30-such degrees in each Sign – this means for most people – that many of their new eastern planets will be found backward, in completely different Signs!

For me, personally I found not only how all of my new eastern planets now moved backward. But, how literally all of them had now moved backward into completely new and surprising Signs or constellations.

In other words, my new eastern chart was fundamentally different than my western chart. Initially, I couldn't even imagine how such a different eastern chart could also fit me since previously, so much of my western chart, already had. However, I was still intigued enough to continue investigating.

—

44

CHAPTER 3

MY TRADITIONAL – EASTERN ASTROLOGY – SELF-AWAKENING....!

"There is no better boat than a horoscope to help a man cross over the sea of life."

~ Varaha Mihira

Six years later in 1977, I found myself hearing about the eastern system of astrology for the very first time. I was particularly intrigued at looking into this new, Vedic or Jyotish, astrological system since I'd already had such an initially positive western astrology experience. And since I'd also had so many years of positive experiences within these other eastern Vedic sciences like meditation, yoga and Ayurveda, I also felt intrigued.

Right away I discovered how this system too is fairly similar to western astrology. For example, it too believes in the same basic premise of astrology which is that "the stars and planets on the day of our births, will describe who we will be and even why we will get born with the unique human personality and strengths and weaknesses that we each get born with!"

I then found out how this system too believes in this same concept of the "astrological chart" and also in many of the same kinds of meanings and significance of the basics of astrology: which are one's Planets, Signs and Houses.

I then discovered the chief 'difference'.

There is a whopping 23 degree difference between one's western and eastern charts!

This means that "all" of one's western planets will now be found moving backward these same 23 degrees. And because there are only 30 degrees in each of these 12 Signs of astrology, this means that many people's new eastern planets will now be found moving backward, into new Signs!

I too discovered how not only did each of my western planets now move backward these same 23 degrees but each of 'mine' also went backward, into completely different, previous Signs. As you can now see from my eastern chart here on page 52, each of my western planets have now moved backward these same, exact 23 degrees and into new Signs.

My western Sun which had been at the 11th degree of Virgo now was found backward, to the 18th degree of Leo! And, my Moon which had been at the 19th degree of Libra according to my western chart, now went backward into the 26th degree of the previous, #6 Sign of Virgo! In other words, not only did all of my planets go backward these same 23 degrees but in my case, literally all of them went backward into previous Signs. I now began to explore and research these very unique differences between my western and eastern charts.

Planets	Western (-23 Degrees)	Eastern Charts
Sun	11 Deg. Virgo	18th Degree Leo
Moon	19 Degrees Libra	26th Degree Virgo
Rising Sign	16 Degrees Scorpio	22nd Degree Libra
Mercury	3rd Degree Virgo	10th Degree Leo
Venus	9th Degree Virgo	16th Degree Leo
Mars	11th Degree Leo	17th Degree Cancer
Jupiter	12th Degree Aries	19th Degree Pisces
Saturn	2nd Degree Libra	9th Degree Virgo
Rahu	9th Degree Pisces	16th Degree Aquarius

Ketu	9th Degree Virgo	16th Degree Leo
Neptune	17th Degree Libra	Not often included
Uranus	13th Degree Cancer	Not often included
Pluto	9th Degree Pisces	Not often included

You can find these exact details in this next example of what is sometimes called one's North-Indian style of Jyotish chart. As you can see here, the symbols that are used to represent one's eastern chart are very different than one's western chart. Though, still, the three basic components of the astrological chart; one's Planets, Signs and Houses are also found here.

One's eastern Planets for example instead of being represented by symbols are now depicted by letters. Whereas one's western

Sun is found as this symbol: "   ", one's eastern Sun is simply depicted by the letters: **"Su"** in one's eastern chart.

One's Moon on the other hand, instead of being represented by

the western symbol of the crescent Moon or "   ", is simply located as the "Mo" in one's eastern chart! As you can see in this example, on this next page here, each of one's new eastern planets are described in this way:

The Sun	is	the letters: "Su".
The Moon	is	the letters: "Mo".
The Saturn	is	the letters: "Sa" and one's
Mercury	is	the letters: "Me" and one's
Venus	is	the letters: "Ve" in one's eastern chart.
Mars	=	the letters: "Ma" while one's
Jupiter	is	the letters: "Ju" and finally one's
Rahu	is	the letters: "Ra" while

Ketu is represented by the letters: "Ke".

I then found myself reflecting on the 12 Signs of this eastern system and found out how they too are depicted differently. These Signs of eastern astrology are represented by the numbers in these boxes or triangles of one's chart. The #1 for example stands for that 1st Sign of astrology which is called

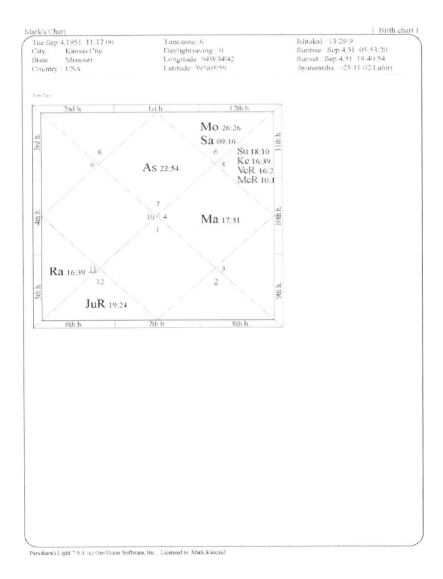

Aries, while the #2 stands for the second Sign of Taurus!

Each of the other Signs from #3 to #12 then represent the other, Signs of these 12 Signs of astrology. The #3 stands for Gemini while the #4 stands for Cancer. I then noticed that my previous, western Mars in Leo planet had now shifted into this previous #4 Sign of Cancer.

The #5 then stands for the fifth Sign of Leo and I then noticed the most significant change between my western and eastern charts, here. In fact, all of my previous western planets which had been in that #6 Sign of Virgo now shifted backward into the previous #5 Sign of Leo! You can find these as the "Su", Sun, "Me" or Mercury, even my Venus or "Ve" and Ketu planets all moved backward into this so very different Sign of Leo!

I then noticed how literally all of my western planets now moved backward into new Signs according to my new eastern chart. Initially, I couldn't even imagine how such a different chart could fit me especially since so much of my previous, western chart, already had.

However, I was still sufficiently intrigued to look into my new eastern chart and to try and see what these many new planetary differences might mean for me. Though, I couldn't find many eastern books that had such planetary Signs-descriptions as I'd read from my western chart. Eventually I found myself going back to those western planetary descriptions but now applying these to my very different eastern chart.

For example, instead of looking up my western Sun in Virgo descriptions now, I read about what it was supposed to be like if I had been born with my Sun, in the previous, #5 Sign of Leo! And, instead of reading about my western Moon-planet being in the #7 Sign of Libra, now I read about what it might be like to have one's Moon in that previous, #6 Sign of Virgo.

I then found myself reading such new planetary-Signs-descriptions as these. For the Sun in #5 Leo for example, I then read something like this: "The Sun in Leo individuals will get born with quite a bit of positive Leo values. They will feel very regal and king-like. They will also experience quite a bit of Sun, self-confidence and many too will experience a strong amount of self-worth or self-deserving, personality qualities, as well.

Such Sun in Leo individuals too will love their independence and quite often end up having businesses of their own and loving being their own bosses!"

I then noticed that there was very little of that negative side of Leo being expressed here for such a Sun in Leo, personality. This quite surprised me since so much of my previous, western Mars in Leo descriptions had included quite a bit of Leo-selfishness which I had to admit, I also related to!

I then found myself reading about my many other new eastern Leo planets which included both my Venus, Mercury and Ketu planets, now all moving into this uniquely #5 Sign of Leo!

And, it was in these especially Venus and Mercury Leo descriptions that I found all of those less desirable though true, more selfish and self-centered, Leo qualities and characteristics.

I then found myself reading about my new, eastern Mars planet which had also moved backward into that previous #4 Sign of Cancer. For example I read such new ideas as these: "Mars in #4 Cancer individuals will be more passive and timid in one's life just because Mars is the least positive when found in this unique Sign of Cancer. Quite often too one will end up being victimized by others or taken advantage of, in one's life."

I then looked within again and wondered if these very different Mars in Cancer descriptions also fit me. The first thing I realized here was just how very different these descriptions were then my previous western Mars in Leo descriptions had been!

I however again found myself practicing that technique of looking within and seeing if I resonated with these new ideas and I again, found myself remembering experiences and for instances in which I had actually been, quite a bit like this.

My first remembrance of being so Mars in Cancer-like came from many experiences in which I had been very timid and passive growing up. In fact, many a time when my mother tried to inspire me to undertake new adventures, I had said, "No!"

For example, when my mother tried to get me to sign-up for a grade-school, baseball league I found myself saying to her: "I, eh, don't want to go….." She looked at me and said; "Are you crazy? You'll love it!" Well, not only did I love it but my coaches told me that I should be a pitcher which then of course catapulted me to the very forefront of our team!

Later, when I was in high school I remember our mother saying too: "You know Mark, you should also take a dancing class." I was shocked and then said: "Oh, mom, there'll be lots of girls there." She again laughed at me and said: "And, what's wrong with this?" She also said: "You'll be going to dances soon so you'll really want to learn how to dance, you know." For me, all I could think of, was how scary and self-conscious that made me feel. It would be years before I'd realize that I had this Mars in Cancer, timid side of myself.

Of course, my mother was right! Though I continued being very shy and timid when taking these dancing classes, however later I also found myself feeling much more self-confident having previously received some dancing training! Later too she said: "Mark, I want you to also take a typing class." Again, I resisted like crazy, saying: "I don't want to go. Won't I be the only boy in these classes?" She again laughed at me though she also said: "You'll be going to college soon and you know with you hand writing, you'll really want to be able to type your college papers."

And, oh my God, was she right, again. I found my many, college writing assignments to be so much more easy and effortless just because I'd learned how to type! By now I began to realize how so many of my mother's natural suggestions and encouragements were completely right on for me, in spite of me having such a passive and timid Mars part of myself. This so very clearly, helped me to see that my new eastern Mars in Cancer fit me much more accurately than my previous, western Mars in Leo, descriptions, had!

I now found myself reading about my new, eastern Jupiter in #12 Pisces planet and how different this was than my western Jupiter which had been in that very different, #1 Sign of Aries. Now, my Jupiter was supposed to be in that very unique, #12 Sign of Pisces so now I found myself reading very different descriptions of Pisces vs. Aries. These as you can imagine were so very different than what I'd read from my western Jupiter supposedly being in that #1 Aries - Sign.

Now I found myself reading such Jupiter in Pisces descriptions as these: "Jupiter is very happy and well-developed in Pisces which means that more of the positive side of both Jupiter and Pisces will be found in such individuals. Many such Jupiter in Pisces individuals will want to be teachers in this life. Also, many such Jupiter in Pisces persons will be more philosophical oriented within themselves and their thinking and many of these too will love philosophers and teachers."

And this was especially true for me. I'd long loved reading about such ancient philosophies and philosophers. In fact, some of my greatest heroes were such ancient philosophers as

Plato and Aristotle. I then remembered how I'd often also loved my teachers and even though I was shy, I remembered too how much I loved being in their presence when in class! This too was quite a bit different than my previous western Jupiter in Aries descriptions which described such Jupiter individuals in terms of being so very active, dynamic and pioneers.

I was nothing like this growing up and hadn't quite related so much to this part of my western chart though I didn't understand why until now when I discovered just how much more accurately my new eastern Jupiter in Pisces, fit me

I now began reading about my new eastern #7 Libra Rising Sign which was so very different than my western Rising Sign which had my Rising Sign in the #8 Sign of Scorpio. I had never quite related very much to what I had read about having such a Scorpio, Rising Sign personality. Though I didn't quite understand this until now when I read about my new, eastern Libra, Rising Sign-descriptions.

I hadn't related so much to such Scorpio ideas as having such an intense, strong conviction and even judgmental personality, nature. And, I hadn't resonated to those unique Scorpio flavors of being a highly opinionated kind of person, nor would I get Scorpio irritated, angry or mad if I found people doing what was wrong, in their lives!

Though, it wasn't until I read about such a Libra Rising Sign personality that I realized why. I then read such Libra Rising Sign descriptions as these: "Libra personalities will like harmony in their lives. They will also find themselves being more of the peacemakers in their homes and environments and also make great judges, counselors and advisers because of their uniquely, more objective, Libra point of view."

I so much more related to this new, eastern Libra Rising Sign

Personality descriptions than my previous western Scorpio Rising Sign. Though, I didn't understand why, until now.

After this I found myself reflecting on my new, eastern Saturn planet which was now supposed to be in that much less positive, #6 Sign of Virgo. Fairly quickly here I also began to realize why I had not previously related to my western Saturn in #7 Libra descriptions. Though, I would have loved being born with such an auspicious, exalted Saturn in Libra nature, alas, that wasn't me at all.

When I found myself reading about what such Saturn in Virgo persons might be like, I read something like this: "Saturn in general, tends to represent those unique Saturn, "lessons of…." that we were each born with. Saturn in Virgo then would represent more typically, such negative lessons of a uniquely Virgo, kind.

Saturn in Virgo tends to represent the kind of person who has many more negative Virgo tendencies like being extremely more self-critical as well as being more fault finding with others. Also, many such Saturn in Virgo individuals will have more negative Saturn experiences too like impatience and a strong sense of delay as well as the feeling that life is improving much less rapidly than on would like. Also, many other typically more unique Saturn negatives as disappointments, frustrations, loses, grief, struggling, suffering and even depression can also be found when Saturn is found in this less positive Sign of Virgo!"

Wow, was this so very different than my western chart which had my Saturn, exalted in that #7 Sign of Libra! Now, I saw why I hadn't related to those so many positive Saturn descriptions which are so much more prevalent when Saturn is in Libra. I wasn't such a patient, mature or steady kind of Saturn person, growing up. Though, I never quite understood this until I now started reading about my eastern Saturn planet being in that very different, previous #6 Sign of Virgo!

As I then reflected on all of these more negative Virgo and Saturn descriptions, I personally realized that I was indeed, experiencing many more of these than those much more rosy, exalted Saturn experiences that I'd originally read about from my exalted, western Saturn planet!

I again looked within myself while wondering about this and then had many such new, realizations and revelations as to exactly how much more accurately my new, eastern, Saturn in Virgo placement really did fit me. One, most vivid remembrance came from another experience that I had, when my mother said to me at some point: "Mark, why is it that you carry the weight of the world, upon your shoulders?"

I, of course, didn't even realize that I did this but now upon reading about my new eastern Saturn being supposedly in this #6 Virgo; I remembered that experience and how true it was for me, that I did have this very same, too serious Saturn sense.

I now found myself reflecting on my new eastern, Mercury planet which was also supposed to be so much less positive, in my new, eastern chart. I also quickly discovered that my personal eastern Mercury was also supposed to have moved from its unique, western 'exalted' in #6 Virgo position into a much less positive, position in the unique #5 Sign of Leo!

When I read about Mercury being in Leo I read something like this: "Mercury in Leo individuals tend to have less positive, Mercury thinking natures and quite often tend to have a kind of Leo, rigidity and fixity just because Mercury's position becomes much less positive when found in this more self-centered Sign of Leo!" I then began to realize not only did my new, less positive Mercury in Leo fit me better but I now began to see why I hadn't related so well to my previous exalted Mercury descriptions. For example, I hadn't been such a superior, intellectually capable kind of person growing up. I also began to better understand now why I even performed so poorly in school and why it was much harder using my personal Mercury intellectual side of myself. All of these kinds of experiences then convinced me that my new eastern Mercury in Leo nature did fit me much less accurately than my western Mercury in Virgo descriptions had!

I next had another deeper cognition of myself when I found myself reflecting on my new, eastern Venus in Leo position. Whereas my previous western Venus planet had my Venus in that unique #6 Sign of Virgo, now moving backward those 23 degrees, I found my new eastern planet was in that very new, and different, previous #5 Sign of Leo.

The first thing I learned here about myself here was 'how' I did have a more unique kind of self-centered, giving, Venus side to myself. Venus is thought to be more selfish and self-absorbed within Leo just because more of the selfish side of Leo ends up being found when Venus is found within this unique Sign. I then compared this to my previous western Venus in Virgo descriptions and realized for the first time, 'why' I hadn't related so vividly to my even more negative western Venus in Virgo descriptions! I wasn't a Venus in Virgo, self-critical loving person. I was instead, a more self-centered Venus kind of person if you can see what I mean.

Though it can be difficult facing such negatives about oneself, when studying one's natural chart, it will really help to also know that any such negative planets really represent 'where' we came into this life to grow and self-improve. Now, back to my new Venus discoveries.

I remembered how often whenever I found myself involved in

my normal Venus relationships, I would quite often find myself "waiting" to give, depending on whether or not that other person first gave to me! Though, I didn't understand this at all before, now, however from this very moment I began to better understand that I didn't have that uniquely more spontaneous giving kind of nature. This is more common when Venus is found moving through either of its three better Signs of #2 Taurus, #2 Libra and especially, exalted #12 Sign of Pisces.

Those unique times of each year when that very real Venus planet in the sky will be found moving through these better Venus Signs will convince anyone, just what such a more positive and uplifting Venus, really feels like! I also realized at this time that the more negative Venus in #6 descriptions which were found in my unique western chart, hadn't fit me as accurately as my new western Venus in #5 Leo, descriptions.

I then finished my new eastern exploration by reflecting again on my Moon's "Size". I then discovered that the literal Size of one's Moon-planet will not end up changing at all, even though one's Moon- Sign nature will be found going backward due to this all-important 23 degree, shift! In other words, the literal astronomy of one's chart will not change between one's western vs. eastern charts even though many of one's planetary Signs, positions, will! I now saw why I had related so well to those initial western Moon-small-Size descriptions and why this part of me, hadn't changed from my eastern chart..

I was now quite enjoying how much more accurately my new eastern chart fit me. And, where I thought that my western chart had fit me well, now in comparison I began to realize that really only about 30-40% of my western chart really had fit me!

Unfortunately, at this point I also found myself realizing that there was this very distinct and pervasive fatalism that was quite vividly permeating all of the eastern astrology books that

I'd been studying. I then found this quite disappointing because if one can't really change or improve oneself than what is the purpose of knowing exactly 'how' one's chart is supposed to profoundly fit one!

The year now was 1978 and I'd been studying my new eastern chart for over a year. And, I did quite enjoy how much more accurately and profoundly my new eastern chart fit me. Now, however, that I was exploring all of these new eastern planetary positions, I began to see how really 100% of my new eastern chart, really did profoundly fit me!

Though, because of that very intense and pervasive fatalism that was also, so very dominating this uniquely more accurate eastern system; I couldn't look past this very diminishing and even depressive mental perspective.

As a result, I again found myself leaving this study of astrology for the second time. This time, however I thought I was quite finished with astrology. I did however have my very wonderful self-unfoldment consciousness expansion practices to fall back on and these were that much more up-beat and positive than my typically, traditional eastern chart would lead me to believe.

If you have any other such eastern books, be sure to be on the lookout for any such feelings that one's chart is "written in stone" and is incapable of being either changed or improved. And if you too have had any such personal eastern astrology readings so far; see if you can't see this hand of 'fatalism' which had been so very dominant and pervasive.

Now, however, try to see past this and begin to try and look at this much more accurate and profound eastern astrology in such a more hopeful and positive of ways.

CHAPTER 4

"THE ASTROLOGY FOR OUR ENLIGHTENMENT"- BREAKTHROUGH!

"The purpose of Ayurveda and Jyotish is to eliminate our pragya parads."

~ Maharishi Mahesh Yogi

In fact I thought I was pretty much done with astrology at this point. Though I had found out exactly how much more accurately my eastern chart did in fact fit me; still that very intense "fatalism" that was pervading all of eastern astrology; was quite depressing.

Because as wonderful and positive it is to discover just how profoundly one's personal chart can fit one, still if you can't really change or improve your stars at all, what possible 'good' could there be in such an astrology? As it turns out this has been the principle problem in most of this traditional eastern astrology.

I didn't really think much about astrology again for about eight or nine years until 1987 when I found myself in India for the first time. I had gone there along with about 450 other people from all over the world, to attend a wonderful, 30-day Ayurvedic course.

I was quite looking forward to hearing about this traditional, natural, healing system of India which is called Ayurveda. And, our first 25 days were quite extraordinary since we had a chance of hearing from some of the most brilliant, Ayurvedic teachers, physicians and even Gurus of Ayurveda from all over India.

However, on our 25th day we then heard these very words from one such Vedic scientist which later I would realize, would very profoundly change my life!

We heard from the Maharishi Mahesh Yogi, who was that most well-respected of all, such Vedic science teachers, these words:

"Uli, do they know the Jyotish?"

Uli was the name of a German purusha doctor who was the head liaison and organizer of our course. Uli then said: "Eh, no,…Maharishi…we didn't think to organize…such a eh, … segment." The Maharishi then continued saying:

"No, they must know Jyotish.
Ayurveda and Jyotish go hand in hand."

We then had a fast and furious eastern astrology or Jyotish course which for many people became their favorite part of our course, there. Though, since they hadn't planned on this before now they couldn't find any formal eastern astrologers or Jyotishees to teach us. Instead they found a fellow course participant who was in fact a professional western astrologer who knew just enough Jyotish to teach us.

We heard from him during the day-time about the basic Planets, Signs and Houses of this ancient, traditional eastern system of astrology. Since, I'd already studied both western and eastern astrology's before, these lectures were fairly familiar for me.

However, nothing I'd ever read, in fact nothing I'd ever even imagined, prepared me for what happened in the evenings. During the last five nights, we then heard from the Maharishi himself about his 'vision' of astrology. For the

Maharishi:……"Astrology is for our enlightenment!"

I was quite shocked and even startled by this most unusual of ideas because nowhere in all of traditional astrology, west or east, has there been such a lofty or most profound of ideas or concepts. Sure, there have been some sense of "spirituality" there contained within individual's charts. The two chief, Jupiter and Saturn planets, for example are thought to be two of one's most important of spiritual planets.

However, there is no clear idea or sense that one could 'use' one's personal chart to become more spiritual or enlightened!

These last few days of our course flew by and before I knew it I found myself back in the states. This time, instead of feeling like I was 'done' with astrology, I now began wondering:

"What had I previously missed, in my previous astrological self-study?"

And "What had been missing in all such previous astrological systems that hadn't allowed one to 'see' just how astrology could be such a profound enlightenment tool?"

It took me about a year but I then did finally feel like I now knew what had been missing!

I came to realize that what had been missing was the all-important self-improvement nature and potential of astrology, itself!

Traditional astrology on the other hand, has long been what we could call, being more "diagnostic" oriented. This means one's typical, astrological chart is used to explain, 'why' we are each, the unique ways that we are. Why we each have the unique human personality and human strengths and weaknesses that we each get born with, has long been the essential focus of such traditional astrology's. But this also means that you will very rarely hear about 'how' one is than supposed to be able to profoundly self-improve or self-develop oneself and one's personal planets.

Though, even the traditional western system has had some sense that one might be able to improve oneself through one's planets. For example one time I read this, in one of the typical western books that I was reading. A student was describing to his western astrologer the fact that he had been experiencing many, very disappointing and frustrating "accidents" in his life. The astrologer then said: "This is because you got bon with such a negative Mars planet in your chart. And if you 'can' discover how to improve this very same, Mars part of yourself, then you might be able to improve this accident prone nature that you were born with."

Though, other than this, there wasn't much other advice or suggestions as to exactly how one might be able to improve one's such, Mars part of oneself. This was just as true for all of the other planets of astrology, as well.

On the other hand, if this very same student had gone to one such, very different eastern astrologer, that astrologer might have said: "Your accident prone nature is because of your personal Mars planet being so negatively positioned in your chart. And because one can't really change one's planets, the best that one can do is to be more careful during this long, 7 year Mars cycle that you're presently, in."

As a result very little is then said as to 'how' one might be able to profoundly change or improve this innate accident prone nature that one might get born with!

I noticed this the most vividly when reading the many, over fifty eastern astrology books that I had. In all of these books very rarely was such planetary self-improvement, even mentioned. And, in that 'one' eastern book that did mention this possibility there were only 5 of 200 pages devoted to this possibility of "planetary remedies". Even way back 'then' when I had the least understanding as to how one could improve one's chart by improving one's planets; I sensed that there should be a much higher proportion of one's astrology books, devoted to such a possibility.

Instead, however, the traditional eastern astrologer then finds himself describing how 'long' this uniquely, negative planetary period will be found lasting. So, if one is having such accidents, the traditional eastern astrologer might describe the unique Transits or so-called Dasha periods which are the classic ways in which traditional Jyotish predicts 'timings'.

However, very little is said, as to 'how' one might be able to improve, one's literal, especially most negative of planets!

Now, that I found myself following this original Maharishi idea of "astrology being capable for enlightenment". I of course, wondered how this might be, possible. I then had what later I would realize would be one my greatest of all astrological revelations!

I'd already grown and improved within many of my personal planets, just from sixteen years of previous experiences of meditating, practicing yoga and a host of other such Vedic science disciplines. This one insight alone helped me to see that such planetary, self-improvement was in fact, truly possible. Now, then I began wondering if there were 'other' especially astrological ways in which one might also be able to improve one's especially negative planets. And for this I then found myself reflecting one some of the other choice, Maharishi ideas we also heard while being in India.

The one idea that occurred to me first was this initially strange idea which went like something like this:

"The purpose of Ayurveda and Jyotish is to eliminate our pragya parads."

Though perhaps you might never have heard of such Sanskrit words like "pragya parads" before. I had, in previously lectures on yoga philosophy heard about pragya parad. In such lectures I'd heard it said that "one's pragya parads represent one's very blocks or obstacles of one's very enlightenment". So, now I found myself wondering exactly how might it be possible to eliminate such blocks of enlightenment.

It was at this time, in late 1987 that I found myself running into some of my Ayurvedic friends here, in my home town of Fairfield, Iowa. There has long been one such, Ayurvedic health center here so I was curious if they'd ever heard of this idea before as to how one might be able to use one's Ayurveda to eliminate one's blocks of enlightenment.

I then told my Ayurvedic friends about my recent trip to India and the Maharishi's idea that Ayurveda and Jyotish could help one to eliminate one's pragya parads. They then said: "Yes, we've heard Maharishi say this before. In fact, everything in Ayurveda from the massages to herbs and even just treatments as Panchakarma and Shirodhara are all there to help us eliminate our pragya parad, blocks of enlightenment."

Later then when I had a similar occasion to talk with some of my Jyotish buddies, here in town I asked them this very same question. We've also long had a very nice eastern astrology center here which has sponsored many eastern Jyotishees to come to the states as well as teach courses in this traditional eastern astrological system. When I then told them about my recent trip to India and the Maharishi's idea that Ayurveda and Jyotish are supposed to help one get rid of one's pragya parads, they then said:

"Really? We've never heard Maharishi say this before...."

I then found myself wondering if perhaps I could figure out how Jyotish was supposed to be able to help one to get rid of one's natural blocks of enlightenment. I then remembered something else that I'd heard over the years about these unique Sanskrit words: "pragya parads". From another yoga lecture, I heard the Maharishi say:

> "Where we have our pragya parads will be where we spontaneously do that which is not right for us!"

I now wondered if there was anything within even traditional eastern astrology which could be described as being related to this quality of "that which was not right for us!"

I then had one of my greatest of all unique astrological insights. I remembered how it has often, long been said: "Where we have any and all of our so-called, more negative or malefic personal planets; these will be, exactly where one will end up doing that which is not right for oneself!

When someone gets born with one such, more negative functioning Saturn planet, for example they will spontaneously find themselves working too hard and not taking the required down time or rest periods that are necessary in their lives. As a result of this, they will then find themselves creating much more ill-health in their lives. And, this most definitely is one such good example as to how such plants will compel us to do "that which is not right for ourselves", sometimes.

And, the same can be found for all such, so-called negative or malefic planets. The Sun for example, when negative will literally cause one to experience much less self-confidence in one's life. And, those who get born with such a negative Moon planet within their charts will end up being born with a much more negative and disappointing emotional and mental side to their inner lives. Such negative Moon situations will then also represent 'how' one is literally emotionally, undermining and sabotaging one's life!

I then found myself reflecting again on that initial Maharishi idea as to how both Ayurveda and Jyotish are supposed to be able to help us eliminate our pragya parads.

I then had my greatest of all astrological insights!

I realized how I had already been growing within all of my personal planets due to many years of meditating and practicing other Vedic sciences as yoga and even Ayurveda. For example, since learning how to meditate I found my interior Moon-nature quite improving! And, where I had often felt quite anxious, worried and depressive, before, now since meditating, I noticed how so much of that more negative Moon part of me had already begun dramatically improving!

I then began to realize too how much my personal Saturn planet had also improved due to these very other, unique Vedic practices. Meditation itself is one such all-important 'way' in which one can literally enliven such an important, greater, internal Saturn, "silence" within oneself. I then realized how much my personal Saturn-planet had also improved due to the unique study of rest and rejuvenation that I had gained from the combined philosophies of meditation, yoga and Ayurveda.

For instance, when I first learned to meditate way back in 1971, as our introductory meditation course came to a close I then remember one of our meditation teachers remarking: "Don't forget, REST is the basis of activity!"

I remember thinking too: "This has got to be the strangest idea I've ever heard!"

Though, I did remember our parents constantly trying to get us "kids" to go to bed, early. I, on the other hand, hated going to bed on time. I, instead, loved to stay up late! I even now remembered quite often, staying up late and well, feeling so grown up! Because our parents too, stayed up late!

After they put us to bed, they'd then turn on the TV in their bedroom and listen to some late night television. I was so envious. And, because there was this wonderful, air duct in the corner of my bedroom, I'd curl up with my blankets and pillow just so I could listen to that late night TV host Johnny Carson.

And for years, when I was in high school, I never had a clue as to why I was so tired and didn't ever seem to wake up until about 3rd period! Now, as I was remembering this new idea of 'rest is the basis of activity" I realized 'why' even this very concept of rest, seemed so very strange and foreign to me! And if you'd asked me, I might have said: "I think Johnny Carson is the basis of activity!"

Now, too I began to realize why it never occurred to me to go to bed early! Since, my original birth Saturn was so very poor in my chart, my very natural, understanding of this importance of rest, was very poor and lacking, in my life. On the other hand, those who do get born with much better, personal Saturn-natures, will find that they do feel to take greater advantage of such natural, rest cycles in their lives.

For example, we had a sister in our family, named Laura who'd been born with one such, more positive, internal Saturn-nature. And, because she'd been born the next year after me, I noticed how 'her' Saturn was found flowing in that supposedly much more positive, even exalted, Saturn in #7 Sign of Libra!

I also remembered now our mother saying at some point: "You know when you kids were very small, when it was time to put you all to bed; it was generally difficult to get you all to slow down and go to bed. But, Laura, when I'd search for her, I'd often find her already curled up in her bed, fast asleep!"

I then told our mother that this more positive, going to bed early tendency was probably because she'd been born with such a more positive Saturn-planet when she was born. My mother of course, looked at me very strangely.
I now began to see how much I benefited from this greater, yoga and Ayurvedic, study and knowledge and wisdom pertaining to 'rest'! All of these natural restful ideas like: "Rest is the basis of activity" and "What you do the night before, will

make all the difference to you, in your next day" then had a very profound, positive of influence upon my Saturn-life. Now, I began to better understand that it was indeed possible to improve one's natural planets, even though traditionally, it has not been thought possible according to this traditional eastern astrological system.

Also, as I continued reflecting on my new, eastern chart and all that I'd previously learned from these many years of meditating and practicing yoga, I began to see, just how "all" of my especially weakest and most negative planets had been dramatically improving even though I hadn't been consciously trying to do this. And, this one, singular idea or realization changed me in more surprising and monumental ways than I would have ever thought possible.

Next, I began to wonder if one could also use one's same, astrology, to consciously self-improve and self-develop our most disappointing and most negative of original birth-planets. I at least now knew that such planetary improvement was at least possible. Now, I wondered if I could discover other, just as important ways of improving such negative planets.

The year now was 1990 and I'd been thinking about and reflecting on this "astrology is for enlightenment" idea for over three years now, at this point. It was at this time too that I found myself, 'aware' of this eastern system's version of the daily horoscopes which this system simply calls the TRANSITS of astrology. And it would be in these Transits that I would next discover some of the most extraordinary and profound ways in which we can use our astrology to help ourselves to self-develop!

Also for each one of you too who are already discovering such self-growth even within that very prevalent self-help moment that is so active today; now realize that these great examples of self-growth are the most wonderful of verifications that you have already been improving your very same, personal planets!

—

CHAPTER 5

THESE "TRANSITS" - SELF-DEVELOPMENT REVELATIONS ...!

"The purpose of life is to grow."

~ Maharishi Mahesh Yogi

Though, I hadn't ever really quite 'got' the significance of the western Transits or daily horoscopes as they are called. I was however, now quite intrigued to at least look into these new, eastern Transits since I'd already discovered just how much more accurately my eastern chart fit me!

I then made my first astrological chart for my very first tomorrow and eagerly watched to see if I could find any personal relevance. At the end of even this first day I was blown away that so much of the inherent qualities and characteristics of this unique astrological "chart" could be found so vividly in the exact, unique qualities of that day.

I then made another chart for that very next day just in case my first experience had been a fluke and then was again shocked to experience so clearly how that chart for that day, really did fit the overall feeling and flavor of that same day! I of course kept making charts of each new days and then at the end of each day, eagerly looked forward to reflecting on these again. By the end of my first month I looked back and was amazed at how accurate each day had been. Then it hit me:

"Oh, my God, almighty nature is in fact, flowing within these exact mathematics of this eastern astrology!"

In my second month of watching I then found myself paying particular attention to what the Moon was doing, each day. Especially since the Moon changes so very often. It quickly moves through every new Sign of the astrology every 2 ½ days. This means within every month, the Moon will be found going through all 12 of these unique Signs of this astrology.

I also found myself paying particular attention to the very real, astronomy that was also going on during each day, too. At the time I was a subscriber to the Astronomy, magazine and they had regular articles each month as to exactly which Signs the planets would be moving through each month. So, I made astrological charts for these future astronomical days and then discovered that this uniquely eastern mathematics was perfectly in-synch with the actual astronomy of each day, as well.

Whereas such daily horoscope or western charts that might get created for such future days, would instead be found 23 degrees off! For example in this next drawing on page 75 here, that I found in one of these monthly Astronomy magazines; they included a picture of what the very real sky would be like. As you can see from this drawing the ½ full Moon is literally within the very 5th Sign of Leo and even close together with Jupiter which was found moving though the tail end of that previous, #4 Sign of Cancer.

The straight line which is also included in these types of astronomical drawings stands for what is called the path of the ecliptic which means the very real and predictable path that the Sun and planets will be found moving through every month as they literally move through the sky! Though, if you had calculated a western astrology chart for this same day, that would have listed the Moon, 23 degrees ahead and most likely all the way into the very next 6th Sign of Virgo! The Jupiter planet would also be said to be in that next, #5 Sign of Leo, even though the actual sky has the Moon in Leo while Jupiter is in Cancer.

I then learned as I experienced these very unique eastern astrologically generated days, just how true it was that nature herself was flowing each day, through this eastern mathematics and was NOT flowing in the unique ways as described by the western astrological mathematics. This means too, that all of you who have only known about western astrology so far, will greatly benefit by discovering this for yourself!

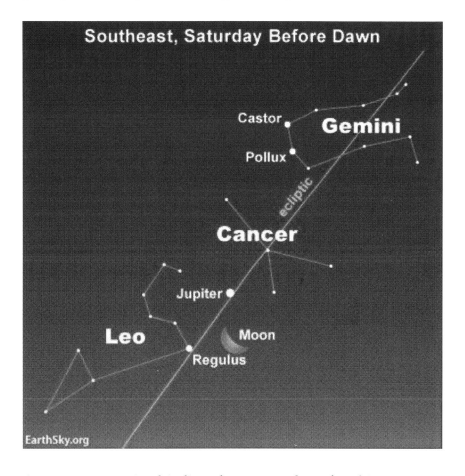

As you can see in this literal, eastern chart for this very same astronomical day, the Moon was in fact, in the earliest of degrees in this unique #5 Sign of Leo, while that very near Jupiter planet was also found moving through those same, later degrees of that unique #4 Sign of Cancer. This is a great way to personally discover just how accurately astrology can be with this actual astronomy of the universe itself. I too spent years comparing such Astronomy magazine movements with these very same astrology charts of each day.

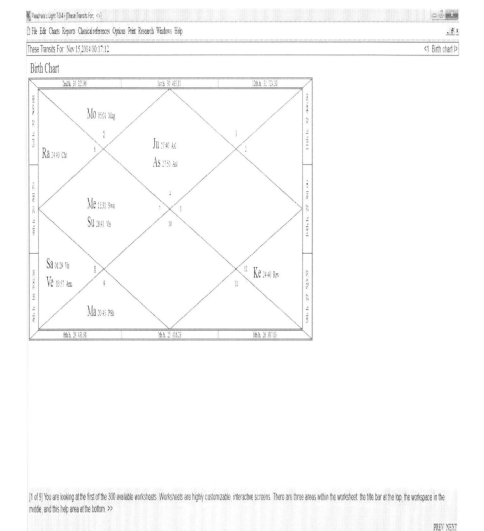

No wonder so many western astrologers are now having such

a hard time with traditional western astrology. It not only has become over 23 degrees out of tune with the "actual sky" but if this issue or discrepancy is not fixed, in another 1500 years, this very same western astrology will then be over 46 degrees out of tune with the actual sky!

Over the next 2-3 months I found myself continuing to watch the Moon's movements and just how different each day felt, as the Moon was found bigger and smaller, in terms of natural Sun light for each day. You know of this already as the Moon's waxing and waning days which culminates with the Full Moon and New Moon at different times, each month.

The most clear and vivid, Moon experience I had at this time was just how 'different' I felt during each of these very different Moon cycles. The next experience I had during these waxing and waning Moon days was just was just how much better I felt when the Moon was found waxing and then quite often, how much 'worse' I felt when the Moon was found waning during each of these next, waning Moon days!

For some very strange reason, this very real, particular Moon-experience seemed to be quite important to me. Though, I couldn't put my finger on exactly 'why' until a few more months, flew by. Then it occurred to me:

"You know not only do I feel better when the Moon is found fuller and bigger. But I also notice feeling quite worse and more frustrated, worried and even anxious whenever the Moon was found waning or getting more and more empty of the Sun's important rays of sunlight. A few more months of this and then one day I had what would later turn out to be my greatest of all, initial "self-development" insights!

I then began to realize: "You know these uniquely more waning Moon-days feel particularly more "inward" feeling.

And, I knew exactly what this meant. These more inward waning Moon-days reminded me a lot about the general inwardness that happens whenever I found myself "meditating"! Then, it occurred to me: "You know, perhaps in the same way that I've learned how to better appreciate and take greater advantage of this kind of natural 'inwardness' in life; perhaps these very same Moon, waning times might also represent such a similar, greater, inward opportunity!

This was of course quite different than the especially traditional eastern or Jyotish astrology which I'd been studying. In fact, these unique waning Moon days are often called the "dark times" of the Moon every month and it is generally thought to be extremely inauspicious to begin new projects or activities during these dark-Moon times of every month. In addition, it is also often said that "those who get born under such small-Moon, waning days will be those who are in fact, 'cursed" emotionally!

I now found myself experiencing something completely different. In the same way that I'd learned how to appreciate such greater inwardness during meditating, I now began to explore this same, "inwardness" quality during the Moon's

Especially waning day and I then realized, "This waning Moon time just might be another such example of an all-important REST and recuperation, cycle!"

Now, instead of just continuing to feeling bad, listless, sad, lonely and even depressed whenever the Moon was found waning, I began to shift into something completely different!

I learned to REST more during such uniquely inward Moon-times of each month and pay closer attention to all of my natural rest and recuperation needs during such unique waning Moon times. I also at this time discovered that I could pay as much attention to the Moon's just as regular waxing days and this helped me to do more and be more outward and dynamic during all such waxing Moon times, as well.

I did this for 2-3 months in a row and then had what later I would realize was one of the greatest, of self-development experiences.

I noticed how much more strong, vibrant and powerful my interior Moon-nature felt and instead of feeling so many ups and downs and sudden worrying whenever that big ball of the Moon in the sky was found waning; I began to realize: "This is one such great Moon technique for strengthening the Moon!"

I was so enamored by this one particular Moon-insight that over the next 12-24 months I practiced this, each and every month. After even a short year, later I noticed feeling more Moon-smooth, more settled and more profoundly anchored within myself than I'd ever experienced in my entire life.

With this initially very exciting and yet, surprisingly powerful new 'way' or technique for literally strengthening one's very Moon-nature, I felt even more bold to explore other self-development possibilities. The next experience I had also involved the Moon and I began to notice how differently I felt when the Moon was found moving though these very different

12 Signs of this astrology. Because these 12 Signs or groups of stars which we call constellations literally exist around our Sun and solar system; at different times of each month the Moon will be found moving through the sky, right in front of these same 12 Signs. In this next picture here this shows that path of the Moon which will be found happening every single month of each year.

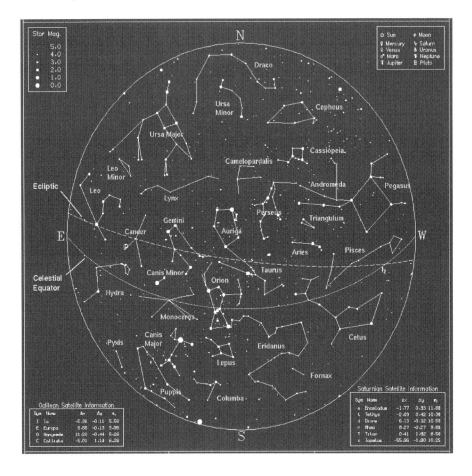

As you can see in this drawing. Each of these Signs or constellations of the astrology exist along a unique 'line' which is called the ecliptic. You can see this line running though each of these Signs from Pisces to Aries and then to Taurus and then

To Gemini, Cancer and Leo. I not only discovered how differently I felt during all such Moon-Signs days but I then created astrological charts for each new day, as well. Take for example this particular 22nd day of March in 2015 day. As you can see on this day, the Moon or "Mo" is one box or Sign ahead of the Sun or "Su" which means the Moon is now waxing. Also, the Moon's in that box where the #1 Sign of Aries is, which then

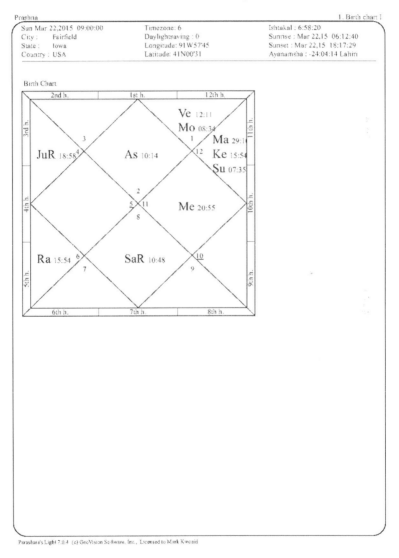

means something. I then noticed that the Moon in Aries felt very Aries, busy, and dynamic which then would be very different then say on such future, next days as here on the 24th of March when the Moon would be found moving through that very next, #2 Sign of Taurus! Since I already

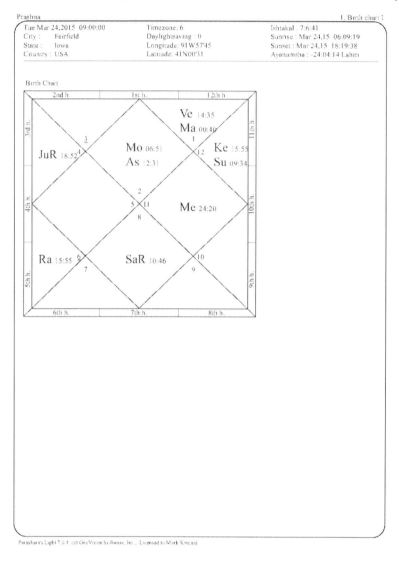

Parashara's Light 7.0.4 (c) GeoVision Software, Inc., Licensed to Mark Kincaid

had such a pretty clear idea as to what such different, Signs will be like for such individuals born with such different

Moon Signs, I now watched and tried to see if 'one' could also discover these same Moon-Signs flavors out there within our worldly environments. I then directly experienced just how profoundly different all such Moon-Signs days felt like and for the very first time, realized that these very real astronomical, astrological movements were in fact, literally in nature herself!

You can see this so very clearly expressed here in this next drawing for that next, Moon in Gemini day. Suddenly, the Moon will be found picking up those unique Gemini qualities and characteristics and literally sending them down to the earth where we will then be found experiencing these.

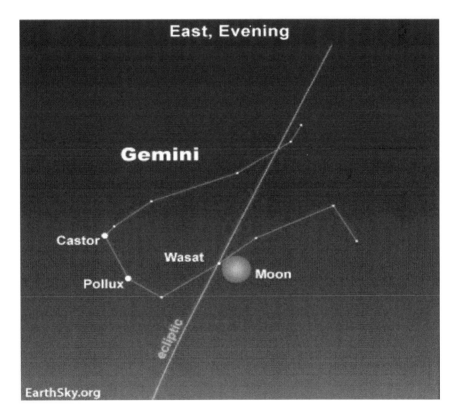

And you too can follow this same Moon movement as the Moon now is found moving into that very next box which just happens to also have that #3 for Gemini in it. This then means

Too that there is such a surprising, "1 to 1" correspondence between the natural and very real astronomical days of each year and these uniquely different eastern astrology days.

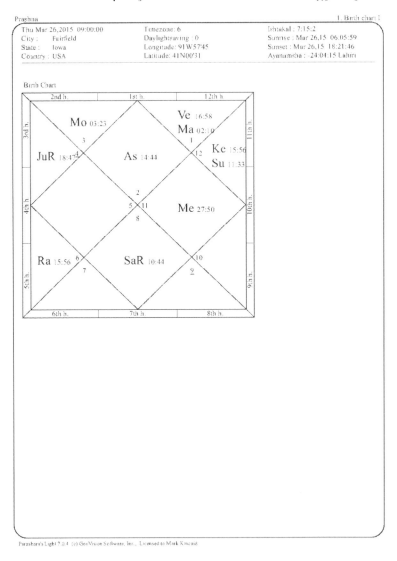

You too can have this very same experience for yourself. Just watch the Moon each day, for 2-3 months in a row and you will discover for yourself that this Moon planet really does "physically" pick up these unique vibrations and qualities and characteristics of each of these unique, even predictable 12 Signs of this astrology. You will not for example, ever find the Moon or other planets moving through other such, Signs or constellations like Orion or the Big Dipper! Instead you will only find the Moon and other planets, moving through these very unique and predictable 12 Signs of this astrology.

This one experience alone, convinced me more deeply than all of the astrological books I ever read! I now knew that this astrology was deeply imbedded in the very nature of life **its**elf. In other words, this astrology is not something "man-made" and is instead, that very literal astronomy which we call life-itself.

After a number of months and even years I began to see patterns emerging and profound benefits and the greatest advantages to be gained by paying such closer attention to such ever-occurring, Transits days throughout the year.

Transit – Benefit #1 – The first truth that I discovered now was just how accurately life itself 'fit' the very unusual and specific, eastern astrological charts for each day. This quality thrilled me even way back then and has continued now for over 25 years in a row, that I have continued to be watching, each day.

Transit – Benefit #2 – The second thing I noticed was just how much each day ahead could also be found flowing to us in either a positive or negative way. In other words, some unique days and cycle times would end up feeling very up-beat, sunny and even joyful while other times and cycles would end up making one feel rough, negative and even pulled off oneself.

Such waxing Moon days for example, would almost always be experienced as being more up-beat and positive while other such, regular, occurring waning Moon days, would end up making me feel more rough, anxious, nervous, worried and even depressive during such times.

You too should pay closer attention to such regular planetary Transits and you will discover for yourself, 'which' times and cycles are positive for you and which are not!

I then noticed how all such future transiting days, also fit the very same, positive and negative predictions of the astrology charts which could be calculated for these very same days. In other words, those same, astrological rules and principles which have been there to help us determine such positive and negatives values within every human being, can also be utilized to discover which future days will be positive or negative.

Also now that I felt like I was being led to this greatest of new discoveries that we're also supposed to be able to significantly self-improve ourselves by learning how to improve our very real, internal planets; I began to wonder if these very same Transits might also be capable to help us dramatically self-develop in our lives.

I then began exploring all such future Transits with this specific possibility in mind. Since, I'd already learned how paying closer attention to the Moon's two, chief, waxing and waning cycles could help improve one's very Moon-nature; I now began researching other such important Transits, cycles. The next experience I had involved how beneficial the Moon felt when it was found passing though it's best of Signs, that #4 Sign of Cancer and the, so-called exalted, #2 Sign of Taurus.

Not only did I feel better whenever the Moon was found moving though these two so-called more positive Signs of Taurus and Cancer. But, I then noticed that my own, personal Moon-nature began to improve! I'd been born with my Moon in that unique, #6 Sign of Virgo, (see page 52) and I'd already learned that my own, personal Moon-nature had quite a bit of Virgo's more negative qualities imbedded within myself.

I was too Virgo self-critical. And I was often too fastidious and too perfectionist oriented. But, now I was beginning to directly experience just what such a better Moon-nature was like! These very predictable Moon in Cancer and Taurus days of each month brought to my awareness such a clearer idea and direct experience as to just what such a better Moon, felt like!

I then continued to explore these in that same way that I'd also discovered how such future waxing and waning Moon days could also be very helpful in improving one's very important, Moon-nature. I then discovered how paying such closer attention to all such so-called more positive Moon times, could powerfully change and even develop ones very real, Moon-nature within oneself.

Perhaps because my own, personal Moon-nature had so many negative from when I was born. It was one such very tiny Moon because it was only one Sign away from my Sun. It was also in that more negative Virgo Sign. It was also in that more negative, 12th House and finally, that very same Moon part of me, was in such close, negative proximity with my Saturn planet, also in that same, more negative 12th House!

I now began to discover just what the inherent Moon-lessons were from my own, personal chart. And since I had been born with quite a bit of 12th House 'loss' with my personal Moon, part of me, now I began to explore if I could "find" what the Moon was supposed to be all about.

The Moon has two chief, most positive sides to it. It can be found in either of its two best of Signs, #4 Cancer and #2 Taurus. Those individuals too who get born with such superior, personal Moons are without a doubt, much happier Moon-individuals in their lives.

Those too who got born under such 'big', fuller Moon-days also are those kinds of individuals who are the most even, most joyous and the most Moon-happy persons. We had a sister named Beth who was one such, most well-developed Moon person. As you can see in 'her' chart here next, her Moon was

Not only 'full' due to being completely opposite to her Sun, but that very same Moon-part of her was also found moving through that best of Moon-Signs that unique #2 Sign of Taurus. And, for years as we experienced here we all so appreciated that she was without a doubt the happiest of Kincaid's in our family. So, definitely pay closer attention to such Moon-

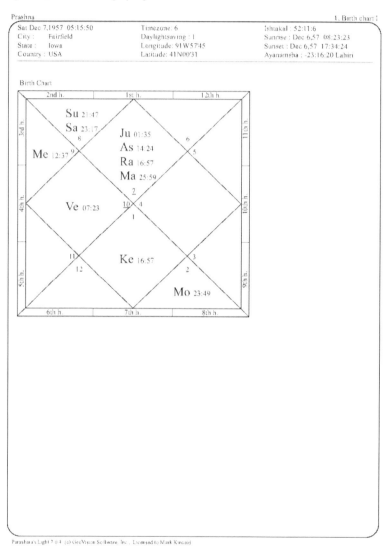

positives both within the sky above and within individuals who you know, (your friends) and loved ones, (your family). And now I continued to discover how I was supposed to "find" what the Moon was all about I then found such an ever-occurring Moon-improvement happening within myself.

I also I began to see now what that unique, Saturn, too close for comfort lesson was all about. In other words, whereas, most of the time, such Moon and Saturn planets too close to each other are almost always described as being very 'negative', I now began exploring if there also just might be a positive angle or possible significance to this.

I then noticed that many such Moon-Saturn of each days, seemed to have some unique lesson there. The first thing I noticed, (see the next chart which is for one such Moon-Saturn day in 1990, I first of all experienced quite a bit of Saturn depression on my personal Moon-nature. Though, then after a few months of this I then began to think: "You know these remind me of those equally as occurring Moon-waning days where I also had such a surprising Moon-revelation.

From here I began to suspect that these ever-occurring Moon-Saturn days of each month might also be important and profound, REST opportunities. In the same way that I learned how to rest more whenever the Moon was found especially waning and moving inward, I now began exploring to see if these equally as occurring Moon-Saturn days might also have such a hidden and surprising resting and recuperative value to them.

In other words, as these 2 ½ days of each month happened, I found myself dealing with these unique Moon-Saturn days differently. Instead of just going about my days as normal, I began to see if these couldn't also be other such profound 'rest' days. And as I did this, resting more during such Moon-Saturn days even if they were coming during the middle of the month, I then began to notice how this equally as important Saturn part of my inner life, also began to improve! And the clearest example of this so very significant Saturn-improvement was that after a while, many such Moon-Saturn days began to feel more positive and joyous whereas previously for months, they had only been more negative oriented. As you can see on this chart for June 11th, the Moon and Saturn were both found moving through that same Sign during this time.

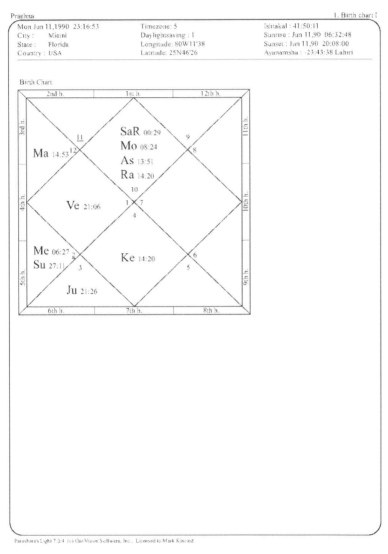

Such unique Moon and Saturn 'colliding' days are almost always described as going to be very negative. And, such practical experience confirm this! Millions of people every month do feel sudden, emotional worrying, anxieties and even depression during such Moon-Saturn conjunct days and yet they rarely know why.

We can even find such astronomical expression to these unique Moon-Saturn times in this actual astronomy picture, below here. The Moon and our emotions do suddenly get affected by this very real Saturn vibration and constantly watching these Transits of each month, will totally convince anyone that such predictable times will be found happening to so many of us!

Since, this Saturn part of us is quite often more negative for many people, you too will benefit by watching this actual Saturn planet from above over a number of months and each of these unique days will help you to discover whether you feel either the positive or negative side of your own, personal Saturn nature.

Though, in the beginning we tend to believe that these purely subjective, positive and negative experiences are really, "out there" and in the real environments in which we live. In true, exactly why we each feel the unique ways that we do, is really because of those so-called positive and negative planets which are there, within our own, personal charts.

So, the next time you find any such Moon-Saturn or Moon-Sun or Moon-Rahu-Ketu days are making you continue to feel rough, out of sorts and negative, don't just think these are typically negative cycles that are out there. Also, realize these are these stars' movements also telling you that you could benefit by learning how to self-improve and strengthen yourself in these very same, planetary ways.

Right away, within even just a few months I felt more smooth and more positive within my same, Saturn part of me, even though I'd felt more Saturn rough, over most of my entire, Saturn-life! These two, so totally surprising Moon and Saturn Transits not only helped me to grow and self-improve within both my personal Moon and Saturn planets but these also helped inspire me to explore such potentially other important ways in which I might improve any of my other negative planets. And since I'd already discovered how most of my personal planets were in fact of this most disappointing and distressing of "negative" kinds, I now had a lot of other planetary cycles and Transits to deal with.

Take Venus for example. It moves fairly quickly as well which means over the course of an entire year, it will be found moving through the full range of possible, positive and negative astrological Signs. Venus, too like each of these other planets has both a positive and negative side depending on those unique Signs that Venus too is found, 'in'. If Venus is found in any of its more positive Signs like the #2 Sign of Taurus or the #7 Sign of Libra or even that exalted, #12 Sign of Pisces; all of these unique Venus Transits will also serve as such greater examples as to just what such a more positive Venus-nature, really feels like.

And since I'd already learned how much more negative my own, birth Venus in #5 Leo was I now began exploring these other times, when Venus is supposed to be more positive, uplifting and especially more auspicious and favorable. In other words, in the same way that I learned how to strengthen my personal Moon-part of me by paying closer attention to those unique times of each month when the Moon will be found moving through its better of Signs, I now began to explore this same idea for Venus.

Those these unique Venus times don't occur every month like the Moon, still there will be 3-6 weeks over the course of three times each year, when Venus will be found moving through these better of Venus-Signs. These times too will be quite a bit longer than such 2 ½ Moon-days each month. Venus will be found moving through its better Signs of #2 Taurus, #7 Libra and #12 Pisces for many weeks throughout each year.

Learning to identify these times and then paying closer attention to such times will also serve to enliven within you just such a more positive and joyous, Venus vibration within yourself. Also you can find such friends of family members whose charts were also found moving through these three best of Venus Signs.

We also had another such sister, named Laura who'd been born under one such more auspicious and glorious of exalted Venus Signs. This Venus planet is supposed to be the most positive and the most favorable when found in Pisces and this sister was indeed both with such a profound, original birth, positive Venus-nature.

As you can see in her chart, next, her Venus or "Ve" was in fact, in that same box or triangle where her #12 of Pisces was. And, since Venus is thought to be the most favorable and positive when found within this unique Sign I then paid closer attention to her to see if she did in fact, have that more uplifting and glorious of personal Venus-natures.

Then it occurred to me: "She had always been one of the most genuinely loving and appreciative of family members and we all loved her for this though of course no one realized this until later." Then, whenever anyone comment about her, I'd make the point of saying: "Her really uplifting and loving nature is because she'd been born under such a more positive of Signs!

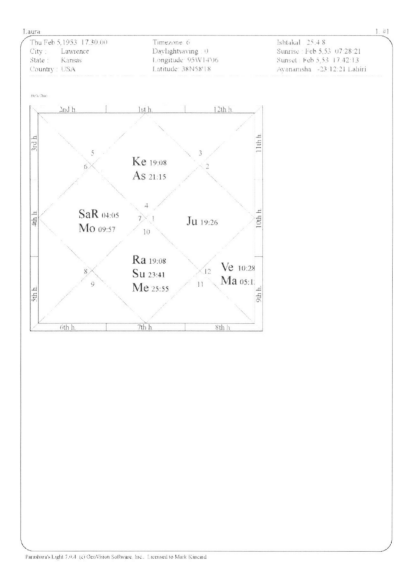

Parashara's Light 7.0.4 (c) GeoVision Software, Inc. Licensed to Mark Kincaid

As you can see from her chart here on the previous page, her Venus or "Ve" had indeed been deposited within that most special and uniquely positive, #12 Sign of Pisces. And, I learned how paying such closer attention to her, I began to much more organically understand what such a much more rich and profound Venus nature feels like.

And paying such closer attention to all such friends and family members who did get born with such, more well-developed planets; will also end up being one such profound way in which can self-improve any such negative, personal planets!

The same can be experienced for all such other planetary Transits. That unique Mars planet each year will be found moving through its three best of Signs, #1 Aries, #8 Scorpio and #10 Capricorn. Identifying then and paying such closer attention to all such auspicious Mars days will also be such a powerful way in which you can now discover how to significantly improve any and all of one's original, birth planets.

Also, you should search for any such personal friends and family members who also have been born with such a more well-developed Mars-nature within Take this next chart drawing for our mother's chart for example. As you can see here in her chart, her Mars or "Ma" nature was in fact, found within this unique #10 Sign of Capricorn.

And as I read up on just what such a more positive Mars-nature feels like and then compared these to those unique Mars-Transits times of each year when Mars will be found moving through #1 Aries, #8 Scorpio or now, #10 Capricorn. I then discovered another such powerful way in which can now be found as that most preferable way to have one's own, personal Mars-nature1

See how in her chart how her Mars or "Ma" was in fact, moving through that unique #10 Sign of Capricorn, here:

Mars is of course that "Ma" planet and when found in Capricorn, that's the #10 number where her Mars was found deposited. I then learned more about how to improve my own, personal Mars nature by paying such closer attention to just what such a more positive and superior Mars, really feels like!

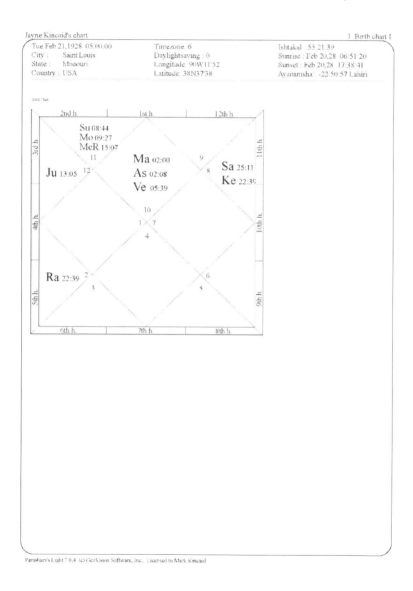

These and so many other, ever-occurring Sun and planetary Transits will not only help you to find those unique times which will be more positive and favorable.

But these same kinds of times will also represent exactly 'how' we can most profoundly self-improve and self-develop within our lives.

And for all of you who would like to experience for yourself just how favorable and success-creating such positive times will be; make a point of paying even closer attention to such, unique days and times throughout each year.

Since I found so many of these daily, weekly, monthly and even yearly Transits days so very helpful for me, I made a point of watching each day.

And what started out as an intense curiosity than blossomed into a most wondrous passion and then later, the most surprising of life-convictions.

Now, have made such unique Transits charts of each day or over 9,000 days I can truly say: "Watching these Transits more closely will also change your own life in such a surprising and profound of ways!"

In fact today I quite often recommend that many such individuals watch these Transits each day as well and most right away find that such greater appreciation will most dramatically self-improve and self-develop, one's especially more negative and frustrating of personal planets.

This new Nature's Astrology Transits which are after all so very 23-degree different than one's western daily horoscopes and even much more positive and hopeful than those more negative and fatalistic eastern Transits; will also change your life in more ways than you ever could believe. Here's a snapshot of one such eastern Transits calendar that I now regularly create for each day of each year. Now, this means that anyone can learn how to follow these great "Transits" from above and discover for themselves that this very same astrology is actually something completely real and not man-made. But instead made my almighty God, Himself!

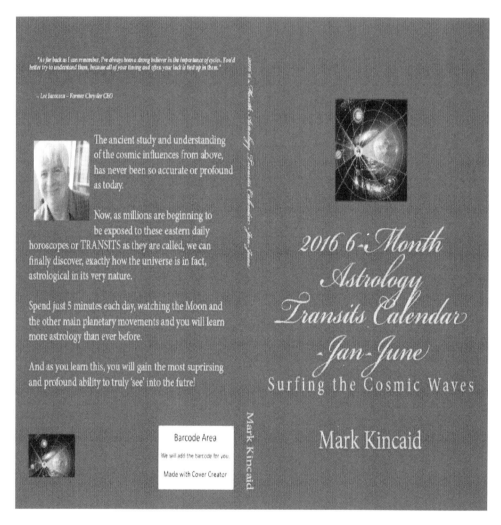

"As far back as I can remember, I've always been a strong believer in the importance of cycles. You'd better try to understand them, because all of your timing and often your luck is tied up in them."

- Lee Iacocca - Former Chrysler CEO

The ancient study and understanding of the cosmic influences from above, has never been so accurate or profound as today.

Now, as millions are beginning to be exposed to these eastern daily horoscopes or TRANSITS as they are called, we can finally discover, exactly how the universe is in fact, astrological in its very nature.

Spend just 5 minutes each day, watching the Moon and the other main planetary movements and you will learn more astrology than ever before.

And as you learn this, you will gain the most suprirsing and profound ability to truly 'see' into the futre!

Barcode Area
We will add the barcode for you.
Made with Cover Creator

2016 6-Month Astrology Transits Calendar - Jan-June

Surfing the Cosmic Waves

Mark Kincaid

Next let's talk about one final way in which people are changing astrology today which is due to millions now learning their own charts. All too now who are learning their own stars can also be considered to be the greatest of Pioneers!

Chapter 6

LEARNING ONE'S OWN PERSONAL ASTROLOGY – BREAKTHROUGH....!

"You all will be your own best Jyotishee"
or (astrologer)

~ Maharishi Mahesh Yogi

And finally, one last most important change and improvement that is going on within the entire field of astrology, today is the fact that more people are now learning their own personal astrology charts....than ever before!

This is a particularly significant 'change' going on today because in the past, the predominant way in which astrology was always done, was in terms of citizens or students going to professional astrologers to 'get' their personal astrology.

Today, for the very first time, in all of recorded history, a substantial percentage of the population is now looking to themselves to explore and come to understand their own personal astrology.

Already this new change is bringing more extraordinary benefits and advantages than ever before.

Perhaps because astrology was always meant to be self-learned but for whatever the reason, the fact that millions today are now learning their own charts, is already giving rising to the most surprising and extraordinary benefits and blessings!

For example, there's a huge difference between the kind of person who merely hears about their astrology and the person who is learning for themselves, their own, personal astrology.

I'd say that person who is now learning their own astrology is going to benefit at least 100 times more profoundly!

This is because when we come to know our own charts, we will immediately become that much more self-aware and from this greater degree of such greater self-understanding, we will gain more gifts and blessings than ever before.

2 – Modern Day Technological Breakthroughs

There have also been two, seemingly unrelated modern day technological breakthroughs that have also, innocently contributed to this great new change where millions today are now able to learn their own personal charts.

Creation Of The Computer

With the literal creation of the computer for example, for the very first time, a substantial number of people in te world, also gained the ability to calculate their own charts.

Where previously, only those who were the professional astrologers and those who were especially adept in understanding how to wield the complex mathematics of astrology could hope to unravel these deepest mysteries and meaning of this astrology.

With the creation of the computer, however, for the very first time, important astrological software also became more readily available and as a result, millions upon millions of citizens today have begun exploring and learning more about their own, personal astrology charts. Such a greater self-understanding has not been possible,..ever before….

And, because astrology is that kind of subjective knowledge and wisdom that everyone can potentially learn from, this most important of changes and improvements going on today, is already giving rise to such a new and extraordinary astrological age and situation than ever before!

For example, because the nature of astrology itself is powerfully more complete and meaningful when 'one' learns one's own chart, this particular change in society, is already giving rise to such a deeper and most profound knowledge and wisdom of astrology, itself.

The Creation Of the Internet

Another just as important modern day technological breakthrough going on today has been the literal creation of the Internet!

Because from the creation of this Internet, again, for the very first time, a substantial percentage of our world's population has now been able to quickly learn about the essential astrology of the 'other', astrology's!

For the first time in our whole, recorded history, millions of citizens in the west have begun hearing and understanding more about the essential differences and uniquenesses of the eastern system of astrology! And as a result of this, many of the most important and vital uniquenesses of this traditional eastern system are now instantaneously beginning to become more wide-spread all over the world.

For example, what one will immediately gain when even just being exposed to this new, to us, eastern system is just how much more accurately and profoundly, one's eastern chart really does fit one.

At the same time, however, millions of individuals, because of this Internet; have also been able to get exposed to the unique meaning and significance of this uniquely western system of astrology as well. This too is already having the most surprising and miraculous of effects. Because for the first time in hundreds and hundreds of years, a substantial percentage of this eastern population is now beginning to look at astrology in a completely new and novel, "non-fatalistic" way.

Both of these two new perspectives, the west more deeply appreciating the east and the east, more profoundly appreciating the west is also giving rise to such a greater natural integration than ever before. One of the chief problems that has existed within astrology itself for over 1500 years is how there has been this great difference between these two major systems west and east. And as a result of this the entire field of astrology remained un-integrated and fragmented.

You All Will Be Your Own Best Astrologer!

Another reason why I also got led to realizing that individuals should discover how to understand their own personal charts, came to me from another idea that the Maharishi expressed while we were in India there in 1987 which is that:

"You all will be your own best Jyotishee!"

And, though I couldn't imagine how that could possibly be true! Because already I'd spent a number of years studying both of these two traditional western and eastern astrological systems and these just led me to realize that there was still a great vastness of astrological understanding yet to learn!

However, from that very moment when I first heard that "You could become your own best astrologer" and that astrology itself could also be understood and practiced as the most wonderful of enlightenment tools; I began to not only think of astrology differently but fairly quickly I also discovered that I could in fact, become my own best astrologer!

I'd been looking at astrology differently now for a couple of years and in this particularly exciting enlightenment way and then one day I ran into a friend of mine who I knew, had discovered quite a bit more about astrology than I ever did.

When I then told him about my recent trip to India and the Maharishi's idea of astrology and enlightenment he then offered to look at my personal chart. I was of course very excited hoping that his greater skill and experiences would of course rub off on me. So, he gave me a spontaneous, very in-depth reading and, I was deeply amazed that he could so quickly and easily express just how 'well' my personal chart did in fact, most profoundly fit me!

Then, however, he finished with some concluding remarks that quite surprised me because I sensed that they weren't quite right. Though, he was technologically right in everything else that he had said. When he described my personality and human strengths and weaknesses, he was right on. When he described the basic human problems and life difficulties that I would be facing in my life; again he was absolutely correct.

However, in his concluding remarks something didn't quite feel right. Later that night when I reflected again on that most wonderful and in-depth reading it occurred to me:

"Oh, my God, I have become my own best astrologer!"

And, it wasn't that I was now suddenly this greatest of astrological authorities. My friend here still knew quite a lot more about astrology than I. Only, now I realized, having learned just enough about my own chart; that had significantly catapulted me into becoming that much more capable and competent regarding my own chart, than I ever would have thought possible!

In other words, as you learn your own personal chart, you too will find yourself that most surprising of astrological authorities.

From this very moment I began to both understand and practice astrology differently.

Now instead of thinking that the power and wisdom of astrology existed outside of me, in books and in professional astrologers, I began to better understand that the real profundities of astrology really existed within each one of us!

Over the next few years I also had one more rather surprising experience which also helped me to realize why it was so important and vital that people learn their own charts. I was now doing quite a few readings for others and one day a lady, named Stephanie came to see me. She'd been referred by a close friend of hers and had a lot of questions and concerns that she was very interested, in.

When I then asked her what she wanted me to look at, she then began a very long and lengthy description of her present, life-situation. First, she talked about the tensions she was experiencing with her husband and children. After this, she began describing the challenges she was facing at work and after this the financial difficulties she was also going through.

Then, I began to feel concerned that she was telling me too much!

I'd already realized at this point that one of the goals of the astrologer is to describe for the person, 'how' their charts fit them. This predicting when you don't really know the person is particularly important because this then the person has such a deeper appreciation of this astrology just because that professional astrology had predicted so much for them.

This lady however was telling me everything and I then realized I was not going to be able to profoundly demonstrate for her, how her chart, did in fact, fit her. So, I told her this and my concern that she not tell me too much. She then said: "I don't really need to have that kind of verification, since my friend already vouched for you. What I really need is for you to help me to both understand and get over these many problems that I've been experiencing!"

I then remembered something else I'd long heard Dr. Johnny Gray, say. You know, the "Men are From Mars and Women From Venus" guy? Well he says: "Sometimes you've just got to let women talk and be patient and listen to them."

I then leaned back and said: "Okay, tell me everything you want me to know." She then continued talking for probably another whole 45-60 minutes! But, then something else happened that I wasn't expecting. Since, my habit had long been, when talking with people to ask myself: "Mmmm, I wonder where that is in their chart" I found myself looking continually at her chart as she spoke.

So, when she described the challenges she was having with her husband I'd naturally look at all of the unique astrological goings on that were there within her 7th House of marriage. Then, when she described her frustrations with her children, I found myself looking at her 5th House of children. And, when she talked about her difficulties at work, I'd look at her 10th House of career! And on and on.

This not only helped me to see that her chart really did in fact, profoundly fit her but then something completely new and unexpected came.

I realized: "Oh, my God, everything out of her mouth, even the very words and expressions she's using are all right there within these same details of her chart!"

And, suddenly I just knew that 'she' was in fact the best and most precise interpreter of her chart!

Though, of course she didn't know this.

I also then realized: So, this is what it means too, why we're supposed to become our own best astrologers.

Because we are already literally living that unique astrological nature that we are; we are in fact, in the best position to understand that very same, astrological personality.

I then found my entire professional astrology dramatically changing.

Now, for the very first time I realized: "If I can get people to speak, then we'll both end up hearing their personal charts, literally speaking!'

And, that's exactly what I did. I began to incorporate this latest insight into my professional readings. See, normally what most astrologers do is that they comment upon the person's chart and then wait to see if the person relates and resonates with these ideas, insights and thoughts.

And I'd long experienced this already. I'd done hundreds of charts at this point and I could tell people were relating very well to what we were talking about. Because as "I" spoke I could see their heads nodding up and down.

But, now I thought of adding something new.

After I spoke for a few minutes I'd stop and say: "I see you're nodding, so I'm guessing you're relating to what I'm saying, yes?" Then, I'd pause and wait for them to respond. And when they'd said: "Yes", I'd then say: "I'd like to now ask you to express in your own words, why you're relating to this?"

And they then would give expression to 'why' they were so intimately relating to their chart. As a result of this we'd both then benefit from literally 'hearing' their most unique and pcrofound, personal astrology,…SPEAKING!

I'd then notice that their exact words, were an even more precise and profound expression as to literally, how their personal charts were most significantly, fitting them! Then, quite often I'd pause too to say: "See, how your exact words are in fact, your own chart, speaking!"

Incorporating this then into my personal readings helped me to much more deeply help others to discover exactly how profoundly their own charts, really do fit them. And, later too when I began putting my thoughts together to create one such "looking up one's own astrology chart book" I remembered this and included this idea of people stopping and giving expression to exactly how they are reacting to and resonating with what they were now 'reading'.

So, keep this in mind now, that "YOU" are meant to learn your own chart. And since you were born with that unique astrological nature, you are in fact, in the most profound position to much more deeply know and understand that significance for yourself!

In fact one of the most wonderful exercises I've included in that new Nature's Astrology book which is called: "Discover YOUR Own Stars Within" is a chapter on stream of consciousness writing. This chapter encourages people to write down in long prose, a lengthy, in-depth description of everything that one already knows about oneself.

Then, to go back and in finding the unique reasons, here and there, 'why', you are exactly the intimate ways that you are; you will then discover even more profoundly, 'how'… your personal chart does in fact, most accurately fit you!

Chapter 7

THE GREATEST HUMAN DISCOVERY UNFOLDING........!

"We need not feel ashamed of flirting with the zodiac. The zodiac is well worth flirting with."

~ D.H. Lawrence

Now, we've covered pretty well each of these most important and profound ways in which the entire field of astrology is today, dramatically changing and improving. Let's briefly review each of these most important changes in these final, concluding remarks of this 1st Section.

#1 – The entire western system of astrology is becoming much more accurate and precise due to that present day 23 degree change as suggested by the founder of this new western Sidereal astrological system, Cyril Fagan.

#2 – And, the eastern system too is profoundly shifting out of that very intense and stifling even depressive fatalism

#3 – And today that greatest of all changes and improvements is how we can now be using our same, personal astrology charts – to most significantly and profoundly self-evolve in this life! When astrology finally becomes more well-known and understood in terms of helping us to grow and become more self-actualized; then finally astrology will really become more well-known for its hugely evolutionary value!

Astrology is the literal way that the evolutionary nature of life itself works!

Section 2

How 'You' Can Find That Greatest Human Discovery - For Yourself.........!

"Life is a field of all possibilities!"

- His Holiness Maharishi Mahesh Yogi

Because you too are one such unique "astrological personality" and also living within this same, astrological world and universe; you too will need to discover those unique ways in which you are even now, living that very special astrological reality – which you simply call your very life.

Though my journey might have been interesting and even fascinating to you, however you won't really understand this until you too learn about your own personal astrology!

Astrology is one such eternal science of life that is all about 'why' we get born and 'why' we get born with that unique astrological, human personality that we've long been living and why we get born with those just as important human, strengths and weaknesses that we got born with.

In this entire 2nd Section then we will focus on how YOU as the natural student of astrology can find that very special and undeniable astrological personality that you've long been living but not quite understanding before now.

Whether you know anything about astrology or not but this book will help you to discover such a plan which will give you the greatest help in knowing what you can do next, to find such a greater Astrology growing within yourself!

And because your personal chart is perfectly tailored to you, what is important and vital for you will be fundamentally different than my chart or life.

In a first chapter here we will begin by discussing how those traditional "Astrological Chart Readings" can be especially helpful and within even 2-3 weeks give you such a greater appreciation and clarity as to that unique human, astrological personality that you've long been living.

In a 2nd chapter we will then discuss how 'once' you know HOW your personal chart fits you, you will then know exactly where you came into this life to grow and self-improve.

Then, in a 3rd chapter we will right away go into that all-important application of this new astrology, self-development breakthrough – which is how you can now create such greater Success within your life – by learning how to discover those unique astrological planets that are in the unique Houses of your personal chart. This then will bring out the 2nd most important astrological breakthrough in 2,000 years!

Most of astrology over the last 2,000 years – has been instead, more "diagnostic" oriented. This means, all about 'how' our charts fit us but very little about 'how'….we're meant to self-improve, self-grow and become more self-actualized in this life.

As we then explore and discover more and more important ways in which we can be most dramatically self-improving ourselves – we can then at the same time, explore those unique so-called Houses of astrology – which will then bring out the unique Success scenarios which will be so very crucial for each one of us to be able to create that greater success that we've always been interested in. Regardless 'what' we've been interested in, now you can discover how Success truly happens!

CHAPTER 1

BETTER ASTROLOGICAL READINGS!

"Astrology is like a map. Like a roadmap, astrology is meant to be a useful tool to guide you to wherever you want to go."

~ Pila of Hawaii

It is of course first worth mentioning that this completely 'new' and much improved astrology coming into the world now, will help you to have such better, personal astrological chart-readings!

Traditionally astrology has long been all about personal readings being done for all who are interested. Whether one is in the west or east but such personal astrological readings has been the very backbone of all of such historical astrology's.

However, there has also been a wide range of different benefits and advantages that people have received from such readings. Some feel quite helped and nourished while some, do not.

Today, however, especially for those who've only known about such western chart-readings; these more accurate, eastern astrological readings, will be extremely more effective and profound to receive.

I've myself done over 5,000 readings in astrology now over my entire 35 year astrological career and when I started doing eastern readings right away these were much more profoundly accurate and right-on for people than all the western readings they might have received in their past. So, if you've not yet had such an eastern reading done for yourself, I whole heartily recommend that you do!

However, as great as these new eastern readings have been, when I also learned to do "eastern astrology" from a much less fatalistic perspective and a much more uplifting, progressive and profound, "enlightenment" orientation; these readings than became that much most powerful and significant.

Because it really doesn't do anyone that much good to simply hear 'why' one is struggling or 'why' one is experiencing those unique difficulties, challenges or failure in this life.

What people really need to know is 'how' can I improve myself so I can stop experiencing these very same human problems!

So, the fact that historical astrology has not been able to find the important ways in which people could profoundly self-develop themselves, then astrology has remained a much less effective tool then it could have been.

It is so very gratifying now of course to not only help individuals discover 'why' they are struggling and 'where' they have their most negative of personal planets. But, it is so much more important and fulfilling to be able to than prescribe and recommend simple and yet profound ways in which they can dramatically self-improve themselves and their personal planets!

Let's now look at one such reading that was done for a person who'd only had such western readings done for himself before. He came to me complaining about specific health difficulties he had been experiencing and was intrigued now by this new prospect of this 23 degree different eastern astrological chart-readings. And also how he could be now improving his very same planets.

He did however have a pretty extensive understanding of his previous western chart and for example, how his 6th House was supposed to be more positive. I then explained that there is also a 6th House according to his new eastern chart which we then began looking at. As you can see from his eastern chart here, he had both his Saturn or "Sa" and Jupiter or "Ju" in this #9 Sign

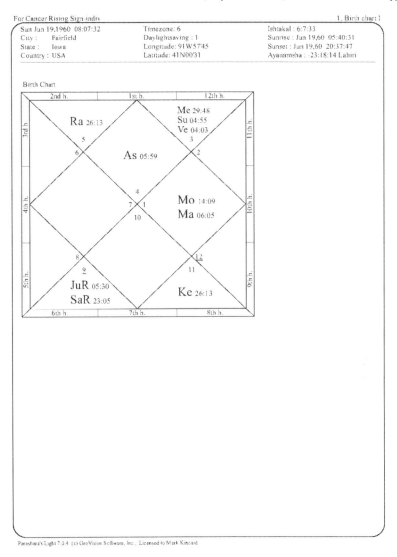

For Cancer Rising Sign-indiv   1. Birth chart I

Sun Jun 19,1960 08:07:32   Timezone: 6   Ishtakal : 6:7:33
City :   Fairfield   Daylightsaving : 1   Sunrise : Jun 19,60 05:40:31
State :   Iowa   Longitude: 91W5745   Sunset : Jun 19,60 20:37:47
Country : USA   Latitude: 41N0031   Ayanamsha : -23:18:14 Lahiri

Birth Chart

Parashara's Light 7.0.4 (c) GeoVision Software, Inc., Licensed to Mark Kincaid

of Sagittarius and both within this same 6th House. He then said to me: "This is very interesting because in my western chart I only had my Saturn in that very different #10 Sign of Capricorn in my 6th House." I then asked: "And, did you know what this was supposed to mean?" He then said: "I'd been told that Saturn is really very positive when found in this unique Sign and that I would end up having very good health!"

I then said: "This is another such good example as to why one's eastern chart is so much more accurate and valuable. As you can see now from your new eastern chartl not only does your western Saturn planet move from Capricorn to Sagittarius but your just as important Jupiter planet now has moved into your eastern 6th House, as well."

He then asked: "What does this mean for me?" I then said: "Because so much changes here between your western and eastern charts, this will also deeply change the astrological meaning and significance for you, as well." We then went into much more detail about this and how his two, very unique Jupiter and Saturn planets here represented exactly 'why' he was experiencing those unique ill-health difficulties that he'd been now experiencing.

I also said: "There's an important tension that goes on between Jupiter and Saturn when they are found together in the same House or Sign. And this tension too is even stronger now that your Saturn planet is found in #9 Sagittarius which is much less positive than if your Saturn had been in #10 Capricorn."

He then asked: "And, what does this mean?" I then asked: "Are you a kind of workaholic, in your life? And, do you work too hard and too often?" He then said: "Yes, I'm afraid that I do, but there have always been good reasons why I need to work so hard. You know what I mean?"

I then said: "If you did have such a more positive Saturn in its Own Sign of #10 Capricorn in your 6th House, then you could work hard but without picking up so much stress and tension. But, your real, much more accurate eastern chart Saturn is indicative of a much less positive nature even without talking

About its added tension begin too close to Jupiter. This means than that you do tend to overwork yourself and not take as much down time or enough rest that you need!"

He then asked: "What can I do to change and improve this?" I then said: "First of all, you need to discover that you are in fact quite often working too hard and you need to create another new, resting habit of resting more consistently and more deeply. I suggest than that you listen more closely to your rest needs and feedback and whenever your body is telling you that you are tired, then REST more!"

He then said: "That's it? That's all I have to do?" I then said: "That's it. Quite often many such astrological solutions are just that easy and simple. Though, because we've been locked into some different kinds of patterns, we end up creating much more inner tensions and stresses than are healthy for us. And, because this inner Jupiter-Saturn confusion that you've been experiencing is also, right there within your 6th House, this so-called "planetary war" that is going on here is also having the most intense kind of negative influences upon your health."

I didn't hear back from this man for a few months but when I did, he had this to say: "Hi Mark, I just wanted to check in with you and tell you what's been happening with me." I then asked: "And, did you find that what we talked about, helpful for you"

He then said: "Absolutely. And what surprised me the most was just how easy this was. I guess I was thinking it would be a lot harder to change my bad habits. But, it was a lot easier than I thought."

I then said: "And this is such a good example as to just how accurately and precisely our new eastern charts fit us and how we can even also so dramatically improve such so-called negative functioning planets regardless as to which Houses they may be, "in"!

He then said: "Well that now reminds me. I'm also wondering if my chart can also help me within my career-life? I notice that I've got my Mars and Moon together in my 10th House of career so I'm wondering what this might mean."

We then began a new investigation as to how this other part of his chart, might also fit him and what this new astrological configuration was all about.

And so it will be for you, too.

Regardless as to whatever tensions or problems you are presently experiencing. You too only need to discover, why.

There is just such a unique configuration of planetary combinations that are the real reasons why you are creating these human difficulties and challenges in the first place.

Also, you need to come to understand these better and then discover too how you can significantly self-improve or self-develop those very same astrological planets which are even now creating within you, those particular human frustrations and problems you have been experiencing, up till now.

The key is to that such more accurate and profound eastern astrological readings will help you to learn more clearly how much more accurately your eastern chart really is. But, of course don't forget, where you also find any such personal negative planets; these also represent exactly where you're supposed to learn how to become more positively self-developed!

#1 – Have such more accurate eastern readings done for yourself but also, do these in a much more positive non-fatalistic way.
#2 – Then focus on that planetary self-development that'll help you to profoundly self-improve.

CHAPTER 2

DISCOVER THE "DIRECT EXPERIENCE" APPROACH TO YOUR CHART....!

"Men should take their knowledge, from the Sun, the Moon
And the stars!"

~ Ralph Waldo Emerson

We should also discuss how these many changes and most important modern day improvements within astrology will also help YOU to personally discover how your own chart fits you.

I also recommend that you use what I like to call the "Direct Experience" Approach to astrology. This involves directly hearing about your chart in both personal readings and such book-readings and these unique descriptions of your chart – will give you these so very important direct experiences of your own chart, most profoundly fitting you.

I grew up in astrology being exposed to this in the very beginning of my astrological career as well as the many 'other' ways in which astrology has long been studied and practiced.

Most of the many books of astrology, on the other hand, are much more about the studying and memorization approach. All of the various rules and principles of astrology can be listed and explained and one can then read about these and see to memorize these.

The so-called "Direct Experience" Approach however, is completely different. It doesn't demand such lengthy studying nor memorization. It instead takes such greater advantage of the natural astrological nature that everyone is already living. So, when you hear about that unique astrological nature like in readings or you 'read' about your unique chart in such "looking up your own chart" books, you will then have the most natural and most unique 'direct experience' of your chart and even remember such for instances and examples of your own chart profoundly fitting you!

I remember when I first started thinking of writing such a new book about all of these most important changes and most fundamental improvements within the entire field of astrology.

I knew I wanted to emphasize the eastern chart because it was much more accurate and precise then one's western chart. But, I also knew that I had to avoid that much more negative and disappointing fatalism and also emphasize this latest self-development breakthrough.

I also had experienced dozens of such traditional eastern astrology books and how almost all of them represented that classic, studying and memorization approach.

Then I remembered that unique 'direct experience' and "looking up one's own chart" approach that I'd been initially exposed to from western astrology books and just how easily and quickly I learned my chart from this unique approach.

I then wrote my first "looking up your own chart" book but using that unique eastern astrology and recommending too, a much more up-beat and positive perspective. That book then became our 3rd major Nature's Astrology books and became the "Discover YOUR Stars Within".

I'm including here on such sample of this book, that unique chapter on Aries – for all who got born with such unique Aries planets within their unique charts. Though, if you didn't get born with such important Aries – planets – then you'd go to that chapter on those Signs that 'your' planets were in fact, born in. So, if you got born with your Sun in the unique #4 Sign of Cancer, you'd go to that chapter on Cancer. And if you got born with a Venus planet in the unique #6 Sign of Virgo – you'd then go to that unique chapter and descriptions of Virgo.

In this sample chapter – each of these "Signs" of astrology are described by each of those unique qualities and characteristics that are appropriate for each of these 12 Signs. Then, in each of these chapters – both the positive and negative sides of these Signs are also described. Even reading this much – you will already have a sense as to just how accurately these Signs-descriptions fit you.

Then, each of these chapters continues with a much more in-depth description of those 9 planets that could be potentially found with these very same Signs.

So, in this sample chapter of Aries – here you can read about what Aries is generally about. You can then read about what the positive and negative sides of Aries are. Then you can go to those unique paragraphs that are related to those unique planets in Aries that you got born with and you then will have your own unique, direct experiences of your very real, human, astrological nature, most profoundly fitting you.

I also suggest one more thing. As you're reading along, then pause between each section and write down 'how' you are relating to what you are reading. So, directly after you read in general what Aries is like and what these two, positive and negative sides of Aries is about – now take a moment and stop reading and then look within and ask yourself this question:

Do any of these unique descriptions fit me? You will then have an immediate reaction and resonance which you then can write down in your own words. Trust in your own words because it will be YOUR own personal, real chart that will be found speaking

Misc. CHAPTER

YOUR PLANETS IN ARIES!

"If you travel the earth, you will find it largely divided into two kinds of people – people who say, 'I wonder why such and such is not done and people who say, 'Now, who is going to prevent me from doing that thing!!"

- Winston Churchill

Now, we're ready to go into the unique meaning and significance of our personal planets as they are found flowing through the unique Signs within our charts. Therefore, if you have any personal Planets within this first #1 Sign of Aries, we will then, describe these here. First we'll describe what this unique Sign of Aries is all about. We'll especially include a more extensive description of both the positive and negative side of Aries. We'll then finish with what it will mean to have each of your personal planets, found flowing through or within this unique Sign of Aries.

Aries – General Nature - Aries is the very first Sign of astrology and in many ways represents beginnings. Those with 'any' planets in Aries find that they like to begin new things. They are therefore, self-starters, courageous, independent, self-reliant, strong willed, as well as pioneers, inventive, creative and strong willed. Aries, like every Sign has both a positive and negative side and the exact planets we have in this unique Sign will therefore, explain 'why' we are found living any and all of both the positive and negative sides of Aries.

Aries – Main Positive Qualities - Many of the characteristics we've just described will be many of the same qualities which can also be described as Aries' chief, positive characteristics.

Most who find themselves living some of these 'better' Aries qualities will be courageous, and charismatic, leaders in whatever fields they're in as well as have an internal strength and self-confidence power as well as assertiveness. The two planets which are commonly described as Aries' most positive of planets will be the Sun and Mars. The Sun is said to be 'best' or maximum strong and positive, exalted as it is in Aries while Mars is said to be extremely auspicious and favorable, positive in its Own Sign of Aries.

Aries – Chief Negative Qualities - Those same unique qualities and characteristics that 'are' Aries, when in excess can instead also become some of Aries' main, negative characteristics. The chief ones of these can include, being too bright, too self-centered, too self-absorbed, too fiery, too controlling, too manipulative and too rash, demanding going too fast and being surprisingly negative.

Now, let's discuss the Sun's presence being in Aries, which is supposed to be the best planet or exalted when found in Aries. The Sun is said to be most favorable, most positive and most powerful in Aries and for many will end up being one of their greatest natural strengths.

Sun – Aries - April 13th - May 13th - The Sun almost always is found moving into this unique Sign around the 13th of April of each year so check your eastern chart to see. It may in fact, not move into Aries until the 14th in some years, so one has to look up the specific details of one's own, personal chart. Now, let's talk about the unique nature, qualities and characteristics of the Sun being in Aries and whether or not one will be found experiencing the positive or negative side of Aries. The Sun in Aries' chief nature is Self-starting. Being the primary, first Sign of astrology its basic energy is one of energy, of movement, of starting new projects and enjoying lots of activities. Aries is a Sign said to be "Ruled" by the other main planet, Mars which means many of the characteristics of Mars are also going to be found within Aries and as a result even such planets as the Sun in Aries. The Sun is said to be ideal in Aries or "exalted" as it is called which means that the very nature and vibration of Aries is so similar and compatible with the Sun that most Sun-Aries individuals are found exhibiting more of the positive qualities of the Sun. Such individuals are often very out-going; leadership types with a love of independence and often times too having businesses of their own. Or, if they do work with others, they often find a way of being as independent as they can be. Many such independent Sun-Aries persons are found too as independent contractors so to speak or strong sales individuals. Most Sun-Aries individuals also feel very good about themselves and also live a very pervasive interior self-confidence and self-worth nature. And, because the "will" is a natural reflection of one's Sun-strength then most such Sun-Aries individuals will have a strong strength of will, too.

There is however a negative side to the Sun, being in Aries. Some such, even exalted Sun individuals are found living some of the negative qualities of Aries, which are found sometimes, not so much because the nature of Aries is negative to the Sun but rather because that intense Sun-Aries brightness is so bright that for some, this overwhelms and overshadows some of their other planets, which are not nearly so strong.

Some such even Sun-Aries individuals are so very bright and therefore, feel sometimes superior to others. Some such persons too can be too rash, go too fast, be too egocentric, egotistical or self-absorbed. Again, however, this does not have to be so. Even such slightly self-blinded, Sun-Aries individuals can step into a greater unity between themselves and others which can then reduce some of their blinding, superior feeling of light that seems to dominate, at times.

Now, however, you find yourself experiencing any of these unique Aries qualities, simply reflect for a moment and then write down how you personally relate to these ideas and descriptions. Take a moment and right now make a few notes for yourself just in case you don't have that journal, yet. Even a few choice reactions here will be helpful for you.

_____

_____

_____

_____

_____

And, if you need more space than provided here than start a nice astrology journal for yourself. That way, especially as you find yourself relating to and resonating with these unique ideas and descriptions, you'll also be able to write down, in your own words how you 'exactly' find yourself experiencing these aspects of your personal chart.

<u>Moon – Aries</u> - Unlike the Sun, the Moon's presence in Aries does not occur during any predictable time. The Moon is however, found flowing in this unique Sign of Aries, every month and stays in that Sign for exactly 2 ½ days! This is why one needs to be able to look up those days, in the past, when the Moon was found in Aries, so one's eastern chart will be indispensable for this. You can also verify that the Moon is indeed found moving through Aries every month by simply looking into the sky and one will directly see the Moon traveling through that same space where that distinct Sign or constellation of Aries, is also found moving.

The Moon in Aries can also be representative of many of the same, naturally occurring especially wonderful, uplifting and inspiring, positive qualities of Aries. However, for some Moon in Aries individuals, because Mars is the natural Ruler of Aries and Aries itself is hot, fiery and dynamic, some such Moon in Aries individuals will find themselves experiencing some of the negative side of Aries. For some such Moon-Aries individuals they may at times find themselves feeling too hot, too fiery, too rash and going too fast, emotionally, whereas other Signs are not so generally, hot. However, such Moon in Aries individuals can still be very heroic and courageous because the Moon-mind gets filled with this uniquely inspiring, uplifting and inventive vibrations of Aries. One just needs to make sure that one isn't being too hot, pushy, manipulative or controlling and you can discover this subtle difference by looking inward now and examining your unique Moon-emotional, feeling nature.

Now, however you are relating to and resonating with these unique ideas; write down, in your own words, how YOU are directly experiencing this and this WILL be your literal Moon in Aries, nature, speaking to yourself!

_____
_____
_____
_____

Mercury – In Aries - One could instead have that other planet, associated with the human mind, the planet Mercury, found in this unique Sign of Aries. This too can be either positive or negative for you. If you are experiencing more of the positive side of Aries, here, than your Mercury, intellectual mind will be very inventive, very charismatic and you may be a greater leader through the unique Mercury characteristics of intellect, writing, speaking and communication.

On the other hand, you could find yourself experiencing some of the negative side of Aries in which case one's Mercury thinking nature will at times, be found going too fast, being too rash, making hasty decisions and intellectually being too pushy or controlling. Mercury found in Aries happens more often when either the Sun or Pisces are also found in Aries. Mercury in Aries too can be uniquely heroic and courageous in one's Mercury thoughts, ideas, even inspirations, communications and writing.

Though, however you are relating to and resonating with these ideas, now write down, in your own words how YOU are personally experiencing this and this WILL be your literal Mercury in Aries, nature, speaking to yourself!

_____

_____

_____

_____

<u>Venus – Aries</u> - One could instead have been born with one's Venus, loving nature in this unique Sign of Aries. Some here too will experience more of the positive side of Aries and find that their Venus hearts are kind of pioneers and crusaders in love. One could even be more Venus devoted to have strong feelings of love for what one Aries, believes in.

Venus' chief, main negatives here is sometimes, some Venus-Aries individuals tend to find themselves being too hot and too fiery or controlling especially in terms of that natural Venus area of their lives where they naturally give and appreciate. Because the nature of Venus and Mars, as the ruler of Aries are so different, some such Venus-Aries individuals find themselves being too push, too heart-manipulative and too Marish! Some such Venus-Aries individuals may find themselves also going too fast in terms of getting involved with their interpersonal relationships as well.

Some such Venus in Aries, heart individuals find themselves being too hot, too controlling and too rash which comes of course due to their Venus giving, appreciative natures, being in this more 'hot' vibration of Aries. Again remember, however, you are relating to these descriptions, don't take so seriously my remarks and instead trust how YOU will find yourself relating to and resonating with these unique Venus-Aries descriptions. Now, however you are relating to and resonating with these ideas, write down, in your own words, how YOU are directly experiencing this and this WILL be your literal Venus in Aries, nature speaking to yourself!

Mars – In Aries - Mars is said to be in one of its best of Signs when in Aries! This is because Mars is so much more like Aries, itself, fiery, intense, dynamic and hot so Mars tends to find greater strength, positivity and more energy, drive, determination, and wonderful athletic abilities to the person. Many such Mars in Aries individuals too will love always being busy and they will often too, tend to be very good at this. They also like anything of a dynamic flavor and want to achieve and accomplish as much as possible.

Though, even Mars is said to be in its Own Sign and therefore, most of the time, more positive, sometimes, even such uplifting Mars individuals can find themselves being too hot, too fiery, too intense, too angry and too mad. This is because the very nature of Mars itself is extremely hot. And, Aries is hot too so sometimes this doubly hot combination can end up being too fiery. Sometimes this is due to other planets not being strong enough to balance this more heated, Mars-Aries nature. Sometimes one can balance this strong fieriness by discovering how to balance and strengthen one's other planets, especially one's interior Saturn nature.

Our mother had one such Exalted Mars in Capricorn within her chart, and she did exhibit all of the most wonderful, inspiring, uplifting and dynamically positive Mars attributes. She was courageous, she stood up for what she believed in, she was inspiring and yet, at times, sometimes she'd come across as being too hot and too controlling. If only she'd learned her chart, she could have realized this about herself and been all of the 'best' qualities of Mars and yet, discover, 'when' not to be too pushy or too controlling. Mars in Aries will have a similar situation. It will be in general more positive than other Signs for Mars. Just make sure that you don't allow this side of yourself to be too negative. Again, however you are personally relating to and resonating with these unique ideas; write down in your own words, how YOU are directly experiencing this and this WILL be your literal Mars in Aries, nature, speaking to yourself!

_____

_____

_____

_____

Jupiter – In Aries - Perhaps you find that you have your personal Jupiter planet in this unique Sign of Aries. Jupiter being in the natural, Mars ruled Sign of Aries, will make many such Jupiter individuals natural, spiritual crusaders, pioneers and inventors. Their particular, Jupiter, spiritual nature will be more busy, more active oriented and may even manifest as being a kind of more karmic Yogi, for example! Though, exactly how positive or negative their Jupiter in Aries will be will depend to some extent on other simultaneous forces, especially one's other spiritual planet, Saturn. The more Saturn silent one is, this will help balance this more fiery Jupiter-Aries nature.

If they are more settled within, then that very dynamic and busy Jupiter in Aries part of them will be able to be typically more fiery, standing up for what is right and all that, only they will not find that they slide too much into more of the negative side of Jupiter in Aries. Though, if you too find yourself experiencing more of Aries' chief negative qualities, then you can make a point of balancing yourself in unique way. One of the ways that the more negative side of Jupiter in Aries may manifest is in terms of one's Jupiter beliefs or spirituality being experienced as being superior or better than others. Other such Aries tendencies as being too self-absorbed and manipulative can make one's Jupiter spiritual nature, somewhat like this.

Again, however you are relating to and resonating with these slightly general ideas, write down, in your own words, how YOU are directly experiencing this and this WILL be your literal Jupiter in Aries, nature, speaking to yourself!

_____

_____

_____

_____

Remember, your own words, your own Jupiter nature speaking to yourself will be the best expression of your own, personal Jupiter-Aries nature. Learn to trust that which is bubbling up, inside.

Saturn – In Aries - Saturn in Aries, however is one of Saturn's most generally frustrating of Signs because the very nature of Aries is so very opposite and in some ways, 'opposed' to the very nature of Saturn, itself. Saturn is that part of us that represents how deeply silent and still we are and as a result, when found in Aries, too much of Saturn's more peaceful and settled quality ends up getting lost in this unique Sign of Aries.

Of course if you're lucky enough to be more Saturn wise, still, and peaceful within perhaps due to years of meditating, for example, then even an initially more troubled, Saturn in Aries nature, will end up being, 'not' as rough or negative as one might expect. Though, if you do find yourself experiencing more of the negative side of Aries or you find yourself experiencing more of the negative side of Saturn, this is probably why and 'why' it'll be good for you to know this about yourself and takes steps to balance and especially improve this Saturn part of yourself.

One day I came across an autobiography for Mother Teresa in which she describes how she only experienced God once in her entire life. When she was young, she had this most wonderful experience which then became her calling and the basis of her entire spiritual life in helping others. Then, she said: "All of the rest of my life I wondered why I never experienced God again and why I felt so estranged and separate from God!" Since, my habit is to often ask myself: "Mmmmm, I wonder where 'that' is in my chart or where 'that' is in their chart; when I heard her using the words, 'estranged, separate and apart', I naturally heard, 'Saturn'! So, I looked up her chart and lo and behold, she did indeed get born with one such more negative Saturn and for her, her Saturn was in this more most challenging sign of Aries! I only wish there had been a more sophisticated astrology in the world for her and she could have been saved much angst and even spiritual frustrations if she'd just learned 'how' to be more deliciously, Saturn-silent!

I too had a more negative Saturn in my personal chart and for years it was the source of much discomfort. However, the moment I discovered how to balance and most significantly improve my very own, Saturn nature, then right away, any and all of my Saturn negatives began, going away! Again, however you are personally relating to and resonating with these ideas, write down, in your own words, now how YOU are directly experiencing this and this WILL be your own, literal Saturn in Aries, nature, speaking to yourself!

_____
_____
_____
_____

Remember too to trust your own words and responses, better than even my own. It is of course, impossible to describe perfectly how each of the 7 billion people in the world are going to be experiencing their charts. But, we can describe enough of these general meanings and significance so that you then, yourself, can finish the job and give the most clear and precise, declaration as to how you are experiencing this or that aspect of your personal chart!

Rising Sign – In Aries – Though one's Rising Sign is not a real planet, as such, it does represent such an important part of one's inner life and as such, represents some very important aspects to one's literal, personality and strength of body. You can even now look into your very body and what is going on there, will be very closely related to these unique qualities of Aries. Look into your personality now and ask yourself if you're experiencing any of Aries' unique characteristics.

You may feel very heroic, dynamic, interested in leading, being persuasive, etc. Though, you may also find yourself, going too fast, being too rash of a personality or too controlling or manipulative. These unique positive and negative differences may also be due to the other planets within your chart, as well.

Because our bodies themselves are so important for our physical health and how we seek to achieve and accomplish all that we are interested in; be sure that your Aries Rising Sign is only found flowing in more of the positive side of
Aries. And, if you do however, find too many of Aries' chief negatives as a part of your 1st House, personality and body-type, then this will be a nice wake up call for you and where you'd benefit by learning how to create greater positivity here in these unique Aries ways.

Again, however you are relating to and resonating with these unique ideas, remember write down and put in your own words, how YOU are directly experiencing this and this WILL be your literal Aries Rising Sign, nature, speaking to yourself!

_____
_____
_____
_____

Rahu – Ketu - Now, we've come to the final planet within the typical eastern system which we can compare to being in Aries. Rahu and Ketu together, represent literally how we each seek to fulfill our literal, desires. If we're calm enough inside, if we find ourselves experiencing just enough, inner stillness, quietness and silence then our desires will rise up within this and be more positive. But, if we are not silent enough, then our uniquely Rahu or Ketu parts of us, may push us to being too negative in this unique Aries way. In such instances, our Rahu and Ketu desires in Aries, then may manifest in terms of such negatives as compulsions, obsessions or addictions, in our lives.

If Rahu is in Aries, look for more of the especially troubling, upsetting and negative aspects of Aries, to be found manifesting. If Ketu is found here in Aries, because Ketu quite often represents a kind of 'other-worldliness' quality, one may find oneself living more of this in spite of the fact that one is also living this more typically dynamic, outward and worldliness of Aries. And, finally, however you are personally relating to and resonating with these unique ideas; now write down, in your own words, how YOU are directly experiencing this and this WILL be your literal Rahu or Ketu in Aries, nature, speaking to you!

_____

_____

_____

_____

Conclusion - Whatever personal planets you have in Aries, you will very likely find yourself living and flowing through all kinds of these classic meanings and symbolisms of Aries. Aries individuals are courageous, uplifting, dynamic and full of such positives and being charismatic, pioneering and uplifting as well as being very independent oriented.

However, like any Sign there is too, this negative side and whatever planets you have here in Aries, if you too find that too much of Aries' less positive side is found dominating, then take this as an important feedback and where you came into this life to refine and self-improve!

I had similarly negative experiences within most of my personal Signs including Virgo, Leo, Cancer, and Aquarius, all of which helped me to discover exactly where I needed to become more in-tune with myself and most importantly, those unique Sign – ways of self-improving!

This first step however, is experiencing for yourself how you're experiencing this unique Aries part of yourself and if 'negative' then aspire to move yourself into the more positive side of Aries. And, as you continue to find yourself relating to and deeply resonating with these unique 'Sign' ideas about Aries, not only write these down here and in your journal but over this next month, for example, write down those experiences as well. The more we see, that inherent "1 to 1 Correspondence" that exists between our personal lives and our charts; the sooner we'll wake up to truly who we are!

After having such personal chart Readings or reading about your chart from such unique and most affective, "direct experience" books – then go about your life as normal and each night, write down in your journal as you find yourself living each and every one of these unique, 9 planetary configurations that you now have heard about.

So if your Mercury planet was found in this unique #1 Sign of Aries and you have found that such a human intellect within you has been more impulsive and rash and too quick to make decisions; now over say the next few weeks – as you find yourself being this same quality – in your personal chart, now make a point of describing these very real, human experiences that you continually find yourself living.

Do, this for the next 2-3 weeks then after this come back and re-read each of those 9 planetary configurations of your chart and again pausing between each of these – put down in your own words, exactly how YOU are literally living these intimate aspects of your personal astrological nature.

CHAPTER 3

DISCOVER SUCH BETTER PREDICTIVE ABILITIES –TRANSITS & DASHAS!

"As far back as I can remember, I've always been a strong believer in the importance of cycles. You'd better try to understand them, because all of your timing and often your luck is tied up in them."
Former Chrysler CEO
Lee Iacocca"

One of the next, equally as important ways in which we can take the greatest advantage and benefit from astrology today, will be in terms of 'how' we can now use this traditional astrology to predict the future. Both of the two historical systems of astrology, west and east; have each had ways of trying to look into the future and predict for us, what will be found coming.

In the western system there has been something called the daily horoscopes which are such a famous and well-used western astrological practice. In fact these are included in most of the daily newspapers and monthly magazines around the world.

And, in the eastern system of astrology these same daily horoscopes have also been there traditionally, though these have long been called the "TRANSITS" of eastern astrology. And, finally, there has been a 2nd major way in which this uniquely eastern system has attempted to predict the future which have long been called the Dashas – or Time periods. This represents the unique karmas or consequences of one's personal planets which will be found flowing back to us, in the present or our futures. These Dashas sequences as they are also called are often listed on one's eastern chart as the "Vimshottari" somewhere on one's eastern chart. There are 3 levels of such Dashas which include a longest Maha Dasha

(Here's a chart for a young girl born on June 2nd of 2015.)

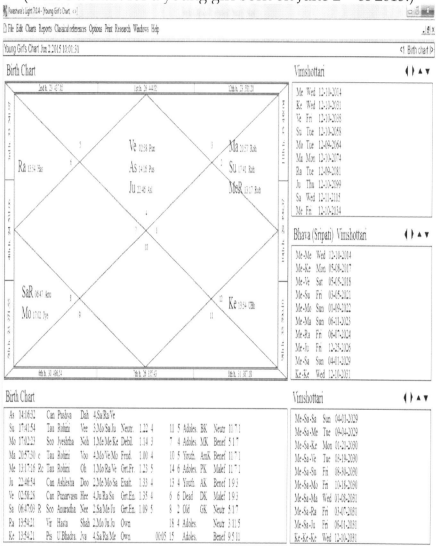

sequence which last for many years. This example of a young girl's chart and as you can see, here was born within one such very long within one such sixteen year Mercury Maha Dasha period. After, this she will be moving into a 2nd major Maha Dasha period of Ketu which will last for 7 years and until 2031. And after this she'll begin a very nice, 20-year Venus periods.

In the next column directly below is listed what is called one such medium range or Antardasha sequence which lasts for only 1-3 years. Within every large, Maha Dasha sequence there are a number of such minor, Antaradasha sequences. As you can see in her chart, in that 2nd column, there are a number of such middle, Antardasha sequences listed there.

When she was born she was born in one such Mercury, Mercury sub-period. Then, in 2017, she was to move into another Mercury-Ketu period which would then be followed by another Mercury-Venus period starting in 2018. What all of these mean then is that the unique positive and negative karmas of these specific planets will be found manifesting to her, during these exact times. So, for example, the fact that she was being born in her major Mercury Maha Dasha period will be significant.

For example, her Mercury is less positive being both retrograde and combust due to being too close to her Sun which means this will affect her future, educational years unless she learns how to significantly self-improve her very same Mercury-nature.

Then, there is a final, 3rd Dasha sequence which is called one's Bhukti cycles which last from only 1-3 months. And, for these, such shorter Bhuki cycle are listed in this chart example, as that 3rd column at the bottom of her chart. This one dasha sequence highlights one such future Mercury-Saturn-Saturn sub-period which will be coming to her starting in April of 2029 and lasting for over 5 months. And because her personal Saturn planet is also more negative in her chart, this combined, Mercury-Saturn-Saturn period might also be very important to pay closer attention to.

Of course before we have any such reflections of such future Dasha periods, we should first establish which of one's personal planets are positive and which are more negative.

So, according to the natural rules and principles of the traditional eastern Jyotish system, there will be three primary planets that will be this girls most positive planets. These will be Jupiter, her Full Moon and her Venus planet. All of these primary three planets will be the most positive for her and will then manifest such most positive future times when she will be found moving through her future, Jupiter, Moon and Venus, Dasha periods.

Her - Main Positive Planets:

#1 – That Jupiter planet that first jumps out to me as her most important, of positive planets is her so-called Exalted Jupiter one which is that "Ju" in this chart which is found moving through that #4 Sign of Cancer, when she was born.

#2 – A second equally as important, most positive part of her chart will be the fact that she was born, literally on a Full-Moon day on this unique day of June 2nd. You can find this as the Moon or "Mo" being directly opposite to her Sun planet.

#3 – A third most positive planet that can also be found here is that very positive Venus planet or "Ve" which is also found moving through this medium positive, #4 Sign of Cancer. Venus likes being in this Sign and loves being so very close to an especially most favorable, exalted Jupiter-planet. This then will give rise to a much more affectionate kind of personal nature as well as a more devotional, spiritual nature.

Conclusion - Positive Planets – An exalted Jupiter nature will be very fortunate and auspicious for her because Jupiter always brings to us that important and vital new knowledge and wisdom that we need in this life. Those that get born with such positive and well-developed Jupiter-planets; will be those who have the greatest luck, fortune and divine help and as a result of this, will attract to themselves that unique knowledge and wisdom which is required in their lives.

I can attest to this possibility because I was born with one such more positive Jupiter nature. Though, my Jupiter was not exalted I was however, born with one such better Jupiter in its Own Sign or in that unique #12 Sign of Pisces. This was very fortunate for me because that helped me to attract that new knowledge and wisdom that was so very required in my life especially since so many of my other personal planets were of that uniquely more negative and dysfunctional kind!

This person's fullness of Moon nature will also be extremely helpful for them because they will get born with a greater interior, strong-presence of mind and even well-developed intuitive faculties just because the Moon represents how emotionally stable and intuitive we will be.

One's Main Negative Planets:

We can also look and see exactly which of this girl's other planets will be her most negative or malefic of planets which means where she came into this life to grow and to improve.

#1 – The first planet that jumps out to me, in this regard is her Mercury planet or "Me" which is involved within a couple of important negative scenarios in her personal chart. First of all, Mercury is found Retrograde or moving backward as it is described which is located as that letter "R" which is found directly next to her Mercury which is represented by the letters: "Me". Also, this same planet is said to be "Combust" which means being too close to her Sun which means the Sun's rays will to some extent, overshadow and diminish some of the inherent meaning and significance of that planet which is too close to the Sun.

This drawing then shows this situation that occurs several times during each year when this singular planet of Mercury is found moving directly in front of the Sun as it makes its regular, revolution around the Sun. From this unique perspective of the earth, it looks like Mercury is going backward while also being so very close to the Sun or 'combust' which means some of the most important significance and relevance of this planet will be literally overshadowed or eclipsed by the Sun!

What I would be doing if she was my daughter just being born is I would then be on the lookout for her Mercury nature needing to be strengthened or improved. This will tend to manifest in terms of too Taurian stubborn or rigid in terms of how she thinks just because her unique Mercury is there within that same #2 Sign of Taurus. As you can see too in the degrees listed in her chart above, her Sun's found operating at the 17th degree in this unique #2 Sign of Taurus while her Mercury's at the 13th degree or only 4 degrees away from her Sun's nature.

#2 – The second main planet I'd be on the lookout for would be her Mars nature which is that "Ma" in her chart which is also in this same, #2 Sign of Taurus when she was born. Mars too is said to be too close to her Sun which is described by the letter "c" that's listed right next to those degrees on the far bottom and left of her chart here. And, her Mars too is at the 20th degree of #2 Taurus which is only 3 degrees away from her Sun which is at that 17th degree of the same, #2 Sign of Taurus.

This means that this Mars intensity of Tauruian stubbornness will also be such an important part of her human personality which of course every parent would love to know about so they can then help their children. And once we verify these same kind of personality frustrations we can then look ahead into her future, such planetary dashas to know when such tensions will be even more intense for her.

#3 – Her Moon in #8 Scorpio – It is also worth mentioning that her Moon, though born 'full' or directly opposite to her Sun, is also found moving through the Moon's least happy of Sign of debilitated #8 Sign of Scorpio too. This will be quite a fascinating part of her chart and human-nature because the Moon will be full and powerfully, positive in some ways; while at the same time, strangely involved with some kinds of mysterious negatives as well.

The Moon's chief difficulty in #8 Scorpio will be that such persons will quite often find themselves being too irritable, angry and mad at others when they find other people doing that which they know to be "wrong" in this life! This is Scorpio's biggest challenge and many such planets here in this unique Sign will bring up many of these chief negative Scorpio challenges. Both our father and mother each got born when the important Saturn planet in the sky was in fact, found flowing through this important #8 Sign of Scorpio. And, both of them had this tension of sometimes feeling quite miffed and irritated when their children were not doing that which they knew was right!

#4 – Her Saturn planet in #8 Scorpio – This then reminds me that she too got born with her important Saturn planet also found within this very same, #8 Sign of Scorpio. So, the lessons that I had learned with my parents also became very helpful when I talked to these parents about this young child, just being born now. Always think of Saturn as important "Lessons of" to be learned. And when in Scorpio very likely such negative lessons of Scorpio will be found.

#5 – Finally, I'd like to mention her Moon and Saturn planets both being found together in the same Sign in her chart which almost always represents another kind of Moon-Saturn tension. Whenever the Moon is found with Saturn most individuals will also find themselves experiencing quite a bit of "depression" in their lives. I had a similar such Moon-Saturn conjunction in my chart so I know how absolutely true this is.

Though this girl's Moon-Saturn conjunction will be found in that very different #8 Sign of Scorpio which means her mental processes will be found manifesting in very different, Scorpio mad and irritated ways. I, on the other hand, felt quite a bit of depression because I was so Virgo aware of all of my huge numbers of human inadequacies and imperfections.

I then told her mother: "You can help her in this regard by paying close attention to her emotional, Moon swings and especially if she sometimes gets worried and depressed. Though, because the Moon is after all still "full" that will at least help, a little bit.

Though of course the real significance here is that even if such negative realities are found; the real meaning and purpose for us will be to discover 'exactly' where we came into this life, to grow and self-improve within ourselves. And, when we do this then all such negative possibilities will cease being such a stressful and frustrating part of our lives.

Conclusion – Once we're able to analyze and discover how all of one's personal planets were doing at birth, we can then know where 'they' will be weak and undeveloped and especially which future times will tend to be more negative and upsetting, because of this unique, most wonderful ability to 'see' into each person's all-important future.

We can now analyze such future periods in terms of both such important Transits and Dashas.

These Transits will be that unique astrological vibrations which will be found flowing to us from the universe or outside. While these other Dasha vibrations will be found manifesting to us all, through our interior lives.

So far we've talked about such uniquely negative, future Dasha periods as they will be found coming up. Now, let's look at those equally as important, potentially negative Transits.

Though, this young girl might be somewhat immune to some such Transits negatives just because she got born under one such Full-Moon when she was born.

However, her parents watching these Transits of each month, more closely will help them to know whether any such future Transits also negative affect her.

If she was my child and I knew this astrology like I do, I'd simply first watch how she feels over a few months of the Moon's waxing and waning days and fairly quickly I'd discover if her Moon-moods are negatively affected by such ever-occurring times.

Take this next Transit chart for example. I'd pay first the most attention to these especially most trying times when the Moon and Saturn are found colliding. Because this was also such a vivid part of her individual chart I'd want to know if such regular up-coming Moon Transits also negatively affect her. On this day of February 27th in 2027 for example, when she will be 10 years old, as you can see, the Moon and Saturn will be found

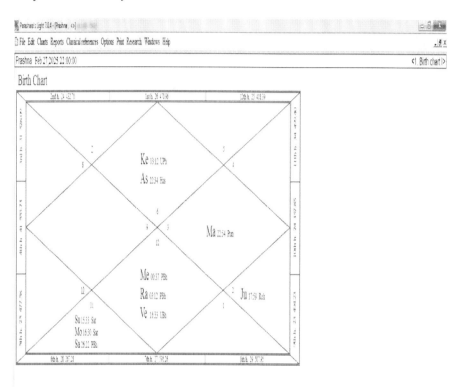

found colliding together in the same Sign. This day and month, too notice that the Moon and Sun are also together which means a New Moon day, as well. So, if this was my child I'd most definitely be on the lookout for all such Moon and even Saturn days and watch and see if she's going to be so negatively affected.

And if she is I'll know just how this astrology of hers has allowed me to have such deeper insights into her and what, she specifically came into this life to learn and grow with, inside herself.

Conclusion –

So keep both of these ideas in mind as you look into both your personal astrological chart and all that you care about.

#1 - Of course as you come to know these essential ins and outs of your own chart, you will gain your first insight into which of your most important planets are "positive and negative".

With such a greater, personal, human-insight you'll then be able to know exactly 'where' you came into this life to grow and to self-improve.

#2 – Such future Transits then can not only be used to know which days in the future will be more rough, upsetting and negative for the world; but now we can much more intimately connect these very same "Transits" of each day, in terms of how they will be affecting ourselves and all others.

I had one such personal Moon-Saturn nature that was so very negative and when I first began watching these Transits of each day, way back in 1989, I noticed fairly quickly that many, many, way too many days of each month, dramatically made me feel rough, out of sorts and even, worried, suddenly anxious and depressed.

So, even though I didn't yet know about 'how' I might be able to strengthen and develop my Moon-nature further, I hoped that I could which then led me to those all-important future experiences where these very same, "Transits" helped me to profoundly self-improve all of my personal planets.

#3 – And finally, one will gain quite a bit of wisdom as to how to understand all such future Dasha periods which represent those unique times when the essential, positive and negative karmas or consequences of our personal planets, will be found manifesting to us.

Though, in the beginning you will tend to experience many such future Dasha periods in terms of whether these periods are associated with one's positive vs. negative planets.

Certainly however, you can right away begin to use such especially negative Dasha times to work and improve those very same planets which had been more negative since you were born.

And, the proof or verification that you've been able to make such great self-progress, will be all such future, so-called Negative Transits and Dashas will no longer end up being negative for you, just because you'll been able to learn how to significantly self-improve and self-develop, your previously most distressing and negative of planets.

As a result, such future Transit sand Dashas might then become a much better feedback as to just how much, great, self-growth you've been able to create within yourself!

And all then who are experiencing for themselves just how much more accurately and profoundly these eastern Transits fit life – will become such surprising and unprecedented 'pioneers' of this most vital, predictive aspect of astrology! To be able to know the future, is an extremely exciting and profound human, natural capability.

CHAPTER 4

THE MOST PROFOUND OF SELF-DEVELOPMENT TOOLS!

*"Don't take your chart seriously like it's written in stone.
It's just the state of physiology at birth."*

~ His Holiness Maharishi Mahesh Yogi

Without a doubt, the greatest aspect of both of these two most monumental breakthroughs – will be how both consciousness and astrology can now be used as such important self-grow tools.

Now, as you explore your own personal chart, pay the closest attention to those planets that are so very much more negative vs. those planets which are uniquely, more positive!

Though, it will also be very important to know where your greatest, most positive planets are springing from; it is even more important to know your weakest of planets, because these represent where you came into this life to grow and dramatically self-improve.

Even this one different astrological perspective will change your life!

And even though much of traditional astrology, west and east have continued to look at one's charts in terms of only diagnosing where one is strong and where one is weak; still it will be very important to now realize, that these weakest of negative planets also represent exactly 'where' we came into this life to grow and self-improve. I was now exploring this possibility from the moment I returned from India and first began exploring this idea of astrology being potentially about helping us to become more enlightened, in my life.

That then led me to this most extraordinary realization that we're in fact, supposed to be growing within those very same, planets which had been more negative or 'malefic' within our original birth charts.

And, now that I was watching these eastern "Transits" of each day, I right away became more aware of those very times or Transits in which each of these planets of astrology are already, supposed to be more well-developed and positive.

There is still category called planets in their "Own Signs" and planets when they are "Exalted.

The Moon is said to be in its Own Sign, one of its most positive of Signs when found in that unique, #4 Sign of Cancer and the Moon's exalted Sign is that #2 Sign of Taurus.

As I was now watching these Transits of each day, right away, even within these first few months of watching; I became aware of three such most important Moon days. There were these 2 ½ days of each month when the Moon was found moving through this unique #4 Sign of Cancer and these also, 2 ½ days when the Moon was found supposedly 'exalted' in that unique #2 Sign of Taurus.

I not only found myself experiencing more positive Moon-feelings and vibrations but I then began to slowly realize that my own, personal Moon-nature began to feel better.

And a 3rd, just as important Moon experience I had was when I began to realize how these ever-occurring Moon, waxing and waning cycles also made my personal Moon, to grow.

When I paid closer attention to those especially Moon-waning days but now, making the point of resting more as the Moon waned each month, that was the first way that I noticed my own, personal Moon, situation improving. And then I noticed how paying just as close attention to the Moon's waxing days also helped me to powerfully, Moon-improve.

I then began to notice how many such, more full Moon days also made 'me' feel fuller inside and it was from these experiences that I began to realize that many such Transits times could also be so very positive and powerful.

After a while for example, I began to experience for myself why even such traditional astrology has long felt that the Sun too has such positive Signs. The Sun's "Own Sign" nature is one of the Sun's most favorable and auspicious of Signs and then I began experiencing how truthful it is that the Sun's exalted, #1 Sign of Aries is also so very positive and powerful.

I then found myself paying extra attention on these two entire months of each year and every year that I did this by embracing such better Sun energies I found such a greater Sun-presence flowing within my own, personal Sun-nature.

At the same time as I was exploring all such Moon and Sun, better Transits times, I then found myself paying extra attention to Mercury's best of Signs. Mercury is said to have one such "Own Sign" which is when Mercury is found flowing through that unique, #3 Sign of Gemini each year. I right away noticed how much my own, personal Mercury intellect began functioning which then inspired me of course to also pay attention to that even more important exalted Mercury time when Mercury is found moving through that special, #6 Sign of Virgo.

Not only did I find all of these special Mercury times to be completely helpful in predicting such future times that will be more favorable and auspicious, in terms of the outside. But, as I paid closer and closer attention on these I began to notice just how much more bright and positive my own, personal Mercury -nature was now flowing!

This particularly fascinating Mercury in exalted Virgo days also taught me a lot about Virgo and how there is one such more positive and favorable Virgo possibilities which just also happened to be so very helpful to me, personally because I'd been born with two most negative Moon and Saturn planets in this more negative side of Virgo, inside my own chart.

I also now found myself paying closer attention to Venus' 3 best of Signs. Venus has in addition, two such important and most positive of Own Signs. Venus is said to be very happy and auspicious even, when found moving through that unique #2 Sign of Taurus and within that equally positive Own Sign of #7 Libra. And, Venus too has an exalted Sign, that #12 Sign of Pisces which then conveyed to me, that highest and most favorable of Venus opportunities.

And because I'd previously had 3 such negative Venus aspects in my chart, a Venus in less positive #5 Leo Sign, a Venus which was also "R" or retrograde and also "C" or combust; all of these most unusual Venus Signs helped me to grow and become more and more positive within my own, personal Venus,

Also I began to realize at this point how certain individuals in your life will also help you to grow and self-improve within all of your personal planets. I had a lot of wonderful family members who'd actually been born stronger and more well-developed within many of those very same, planets where I'd been born extremely deficient and not very well-developed.

My sister Laura for example had been born with two important, more positive planets; both an exalted Venus and Saturn planets and since both of these planets were quite deficient and much more negative within my own chart, I found her chart and human-nature to be quite helpful in terms of helping me to 'see' more clearly just what such better Venus and Saturn planets could be like.

So, in addition to following such unique Transits of each year which are found flowing in these better of planetary Signs, also complement these Transits 'watching' by finding and paying closer attention to those friends and family members who were especially born in those better planetary-Signs that you were 'not' born so auspiciously in.

Though, I now knew that I did at least have two positive planets which I could then share with them. My Jupiter was found in that #12 Sign of Pisces, (page 52) and also more positive with my Sun nature which was in that better, #5 Sign of Leo. All such future Sun Transits which were supposed to be more positive especially in this same, #5 Sign of Leo, also helped me to see, not only that I had been born with one such better Sun nature. But, these very same Sun-Leo months also helped me to see why all of my other Leo planets, weren't that positive or favorable in this same Sign. And, many such individuals in the world will find such mixed messages going on within their own charts. Many others too will benefit by learning to distinguish between the 'good' planets in such Signs and those other planets that might be much less positive within these Signs.

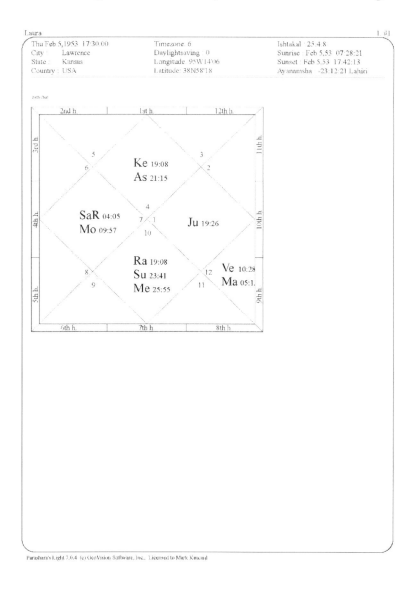

Here's that chart of my sister's who'd been born with those two most favorable and positive of Venus and Saturn planets. You too will find both family members and friends who also got born with such more positive planets which you too can derive such wonderful, greater advantage of.

There are also such unique Mars times of each year when this big ball of Mars above will be found moving through its two "Own Signs" of either #1 Aries or #10 Capricorn. Also, Mars has an exalted Sign which is that unique #10 Sign of Capricorn. And, Mars will be found moving through all 3 of these best of Signs every year for at least 3-6 weeks each year. Pay closer attention to these unique times and you will know more deeply just what such a better and more positive Mars-nature, feels like!

This was one of the greatest planetary improvements I had. And perhaps it was because I was born with the worst of Mars-natures since mine was in that least positive #4 Signs of Cancer. Watching Mars then each and every year, helped me to find such delicious examples as to just how positive and favorable Mars could be. This is also so very significant because so many people in the world are only flowing through more of the negative side of Mars!

Then, there are those unique Signs that both of those two slowest moving of planets, Jupiter and Saturn will be found most positive.

Jupiter has two such, more favorable "Own Signs" of #9 Sagittarius and #12 Pisces. Jupiter too has one exalted #4 Sign of Cancer which represents when such a divine Jupiter-nature will be the most positive and favorable. I first watched Jupiter moving through its better, Own Signs of #12 Pisces, 12 years ago in 2002 which then helped me more clearly, how to grow and self-improve within my own Jupiter nature, just because I had not been born with such an auspicious or exalted of Jupiter-planets within my own chart.

I had a similar experience with Saturn. Though, because Saturn moves so very slowly, it takes in fact, 30 years to go through all 12 Signs whereas the Moon, on the other hand, moves through all 12 Signs, each and every month!

Fortunately, by the time that Saturn's exalted Sign of #7 Libra came up in 2011, I'd at least been watching these Transits of each day for over 22 years. Though, I hadn't directly experienced such positive Saturn Signs so clearly before, I was however, very well-prepared to at least now, take such greater advantage.

The very moment when Saturn first stepped into exalted #7 Libra on November 15th of 2011, I felt immediately such a more positive Saturn vibration than ever before. And, perhaps because I'd also been watching him over much of the last 22 years, I was also quite primed to be able to better appreciate now, his highest and most auspicious of life-vibrations.

This then eventually became the basis of me finally feeling ready to write my definitive of Saturn books which was most importantly about Saturn's highest and most positive of possibilities. That book is now out and is called "Saturn is Shiva". In many ways this will be most people's most important planets to improve because we live in one such, most negative and disappointing of Saturn ages.

Conclusion – Find those unique Transits and individuals who got born with these better of planetary Signs and all of these will help you to grow and become more self-developed within your own personal planets which will then benefit you in innumerable and most profoundly positive ways!

CHAPTER 5

ELIMINATING HOW WE SABOTAGE & UNDERMINE OUR LIVES !

"Is a co-worker undermining your work?"

~ University of Minnesota – Study

We'll even find that such classic, modern day frustrations as how we sabotage and undermine – will be found most profoundly eliminated through both such consciousness and astrology tools, techniques and technologies.

Whether we are thinking in terms of our children and how certain experiences can subvert and undermine their future lives or such psychological practices as helping adults get over such previous negative experiences that they experienced when they were young; we do believe today that individuals do sabotage and undermine their lives.

Those young children for example who get either abused or neglected when they are young, do in fact, take these rather disappointing and frustrating experiences to their future lives!

We also know how such classically negative experiences of losing one or both of our parents at such a young age, will also seriously, undermine and sabotage one's very life in the future.

Why even today, we also know that such modern day experiences like being in the most recent wars in Iraq and in Afghanistan are also responsible for such post-traumatic stress disorders or PTSD's as they are called. These very negative experiences not only cause a lot of personal tension and stress in our lives but these very same, negatives also end up powerfully undermining and sabotaging our present and future lives, as well!

Traditional astrology however, has always had a deeper appreciation and understanding in these regards. For example, the very real reasons we have the uniquely negative experiences we have is because of those so-called more negative planets in our initial, birth charts. My personal mother never learned this and as a result often blamed 'life' for this situation where her mother died at a very early age and she had to grow up with that most disappointing situation of not having that all-important motherly influence in her early life!

Though, I began to understand this situation better when I came to understand her personal chart. As you can see in that chart of hers that is listed her on page 145, you can find that clear reason why she'd been born without a mother!

She got born literally, on a new Moon day when the Sun and Moon are both found in the same Sign. This means than that one's very Moon-nature would be sorely, negatively affected and that many of the natural meanings and symbolisms of the Moon will also be found more deficient or negative within one's life

She would first of all experience much 'loss' of mother in her life. She experienced this the most vividly because of that so-called negative Moon-configuration in her chart. Though, not knowing this and not being taught this in her life she ended up spending quite a bit of her life struggling and suffering in this unique way just because she had not been led to really understand what was going on.

Everyone then has such unique ways in which we all end up sabotaging and undermining our very lives which are in fact, due to those very negative planets which are right there in our personal astrological charts.

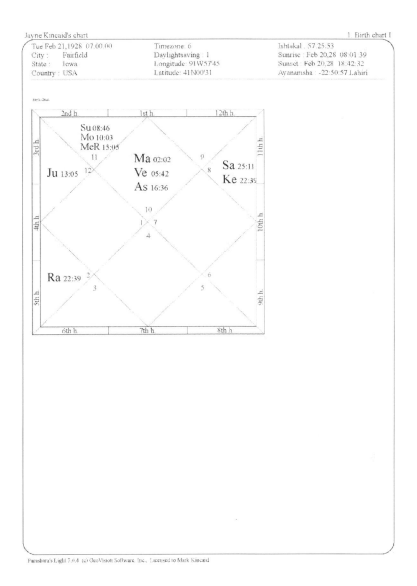

I too got born then in a life-situation where I got born with a mother who couldn't be as Moon giving, caring or even motherly as I would have liked. And, like my mother, I too spent many of my earliest of years sad and frustrated in my life that my mother hadn't quite been there for me! Though, don't get me wrong, our mother was a great lady and gave to us in

151

other ways. She also had that exalted Mars in #10 Capricorn nature and that very positive, Jupiter, spirituality due to being in that #12 Sign of Pisces! And we all benefited from her due to these important, more positive of birth-planets. However, she still struggled emotionally. And I too struggled emotionally for many years until one day I began to understand my Moon!

Even my western chart (page 39) helped me to begin to understand my Moon's great, personal weakness. Even in 1970 when I first learned about my small-Moon nature and all that would mean; I began looking for unique ways in which I might strengthen this part of myself.

That then led me to meditating and to what ended up being one of the greatest of Moon self-development techniques which was learning to meditate. In fact, from the very moment I first learned to meditate in 1971 I began to Moon feel better!

And that all-important Moon growth continued year after year, after year.

Sixteen years later however, in 1987 when I came back from India where I heard how astrology is supposed to be able to help us to become more enlightened; I began to understand more clearly that one can in fact, powerfully improve and strengthen all of one's especially most negative of personal planets!

Then, over the next few years as I learned how to significantly, self-improve my very own personal Moon nature even more, I found myself growing more in terms of my Moon-nature than ever before! For example, when I learned from my eastern chart, (see page 52) that my Moon being in my 12th House and in such close proximity to my Saturn nature, was so very negative in my chart; this then helped me to see exactly 'why' and 'how' I emotionally undermined and sabotaged my life!

Later, however as I began to learn how to powerfully self-improve and self-develop myself in this all-important Moon way; I not only began to feel Moon better but I then began to notice that I stopped blaming my mother for well, anything! That not only improved my inner life but that also ended up improving my intimate relationship with my mother

The last fifteen years of my mother's life were some of the happiest years of my life because I had now learned how to stop undermining and sabotaging my life in terms of this Moon, motherly part of my inner life.

Just know now that every single way in which every single human being ends up sabotaging and undermining their lives can in fact, be found due to those very same, Negative planets in which they were born with.

A lack of human self-confidence then can be found in one such negative Sun planets within our charts.

Emotional and mental problems can also be traced to those very same, so-called negative Moon-configurations within our charts.

Health problems? Even many today are bringing out this great truth that ill-health is created quite often by the person themselves. Why a person over works or doesn't take adequate care of themselves and therefore, undermines and sabotages their very health, can also be found in these unique negative planets within their charts.

Romantic and relationship problems too can be found in the unique "negative" planetary Venus and Mars planetary configurations found within everyone's charts.

Family problems and difficulties in the home can also be found in those very same, negative personal planets which are also found right there within these details of each person's chart.

Let's now take one such example of a lady's chart who came to me with very unique human difficulties and frustrations she's been experiencing in her life. One of her greatest of all frustrations was the fact that her father had divorced her mother and "abandoned" her family when she was at a very early age. Of course this happens to a lot of children nowadays but for this lady, this bothered her the most!

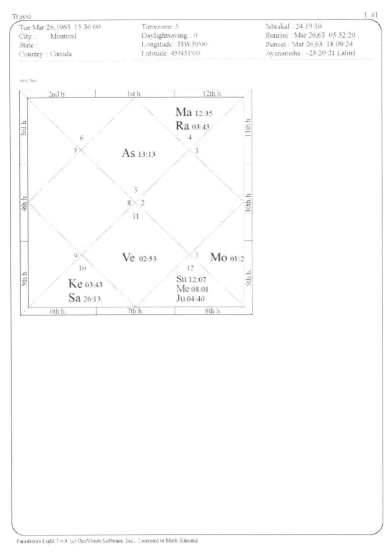

I then explained to her how there were both so-called positive and negative planets found within our individual charts and these especially negative planets would represent not only where our human weaknesses are but why we will even blame others. I then said: "So, it's helpful looking into your chart, to find one such very negative Sun-planet due to its position in this 8th House of death as you can see. This means that you would have the very important karma of a father who would either physically die early or leave the family.

She then said: "That's amazing. I would never have guessed that such horrible experiences could be predicted."

I then said: "Even this traditional eastern system has long been able to predict where such negative experiences will happen to us and how these will so clearly undermine and sabotage our future lives."

We then went into much detail about what she could be doing to strengthen and improve this all-important Sun part of her inner life. And, I knew that if she could do this then she would end up ceasing to undermine and sabotage herself in this way, just because she would end up being stronger and more self-actualized in this vital Sun part of herself.

She then asked: "Can you find other reasons why I also have been so very shy and why these kinds of experiences would so negative affect me, in my life?"

We then explored all of her chief, most negative planets including her small Moon nature which was only one Sign away from her Sun and her Mars and Rahu planets which were also supposed to be more negative being in her 12th House in her chart.

Though it can be depressing hearing of any such negatives from our charts, if we can also discover that these very negative planets also represent where we came into this life to grow and self-improve then this will us to not be shy in examining any such weaker or negative of personal planets. We covered many new and exciting ways in which she could be strengthening those particularly most negative planets within her chart and thus, eliminating how she had been undermining and sabotaging her life.

She then said: "You know Mark, if you'd ever told me that I could get over this particular negative experience I'd had with my father I would never have thought this to be possible. I so often blamed him for that tremendous loss quality that I felt, but from the very moment when you helped me to see that this was really due to my very own, more negative Sun, planet I began to feel better!

And also those very specific and detailed techniques which you shared with me as to just 'how' I could most profoundly improve this natural, Sun-part of me, has already helped more than any previous self-help work I have ever done!"

Conclusion:

Just remember wherever you personally have any of your personal planets, these will represent where you are even right now, undermining and sabotaging YOUR life even if you have the best of intentions.

Now, however, that more of this inherent self-development nature and potential of astrology is being explored and understood; we can now discover exactly how we can all, cease to undermine and sabotage our very lives.

Because this sense of undermining and sabotaging is so much more clear and understood in our society today, this great, new advantage of this new astrology coming into the world now, will be one of the greatest benefits and advantages for us all.

CHAPTER 6

MY GREATEST ASTROLOGICAL AHA.... AND ...REALIZATION.....!!!

*"Men should take their knowledge, from the Sun, the Moon
And the stars!"*

Ralph Waldo Emerson

Now, that we're talking about these unique ways in which we can significantly self-improve and self-develop ourselves by learning how to most profoundly self-improve our very same, even most negative of planets; I'd like to also include one of the greatest insights one can also gain.

Looking back now over my entire astrological career, it appears to me that the greatest thing I've discovered is related to those very same, so-called negative planetary configurations within our charts.

Where these have traditionally been used to explain where we each will get born negative and underdeveloped and now, why we will be undermining and sabotaging our lives; we can now begin to understand how **"these very same, negative planets can also represent that exact, new knowledge and wisdom that we came into this life to find and to grow with"**!

For example, take any such planetary configuration which had been found as being representative of some area of our human weaknesses that we each got born with and which we have long been experiencing in our lives.

For example, in my chart I had so many, so-called negative planetary weaknesses to choose from. Out of all of my potentially 9 basic planets, literally 7 of these were thought to be deeply negative or dysfunctional in my chart and life!

Even after an initial run through my chart I found out how these so-called negative planets really did fit my most sad and

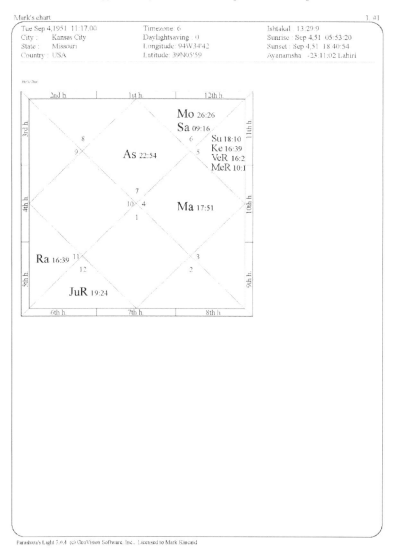

distressing, human weaknesses that I'd been born with. For example….

#1 – My Moon in the 12th House was thought to be one of my chief, human weaknesses. Even those details like being in the 12th House and so close to Saturn and also being so very tiny, in sunlight due to only being one Sign away from my Sun which was in the preceding box or Sign; were all the main ways in which such Moon-negatively were to be found!

And I certainly found this to be true in my inner life. I was in fact, born with a very shy, self-conscious and constantly worrying, anxious and even depressive personality growing up!

#2 – My Saturn too in this same, 12th House of "Loss" as it is called helped me see that I'd also been born at loss to the natural, most positive aspects of Saturn. I instead found that I related very closely to the many so-called negative qualities and characteristics of Saturn. These included….that….

I was more tired and out of balance, in my life.
I quite often too experienced quite a bit of stress.
I felt quite a bit of dis-ease.
I also noticed feeling quite a bit of loss in life. Saturn is after all the primary planet of loss, for us. Those with such uniquely positioned Saturn's will find that they experience quite a bit of 'loss' in terms of career, family relations, money, health; you name it.
I also experienced quite a bit of delay and frustrations in my life.
One tends to be more impatient too if Saturn is 'negative'.
One will also experience quite a bit of ups and downs.
One will experience too quite a bit of disappointment as well as struggling and suffering in one's life.
And, finally one can even experience quite a bit of depression!

Since I related so very much to literally all of these very much more negative qualities and characteristics of Saturn I then found myself thinking: "Saturn is very definitely one of my other just as important negative planets."

#3, #4, & #5 – My many Leo planets. From the very moment too that I found myself reading about my many simultaneous Leo planets I found too that I was living much of the so-called negative side of Leo as well. Though because I also had my Sun in Leo here too, this helped me see that I also had some of the more positive side of Leo, flowing within my personal life, too.

Leo's Positive & Negative Sides:

Negatives: - Being more selfish, self-centered and self-absorbed in one's life.

Leo's Positives: - Being more self-referral, self-confident, self-sufficient and independent in one's life, as well.

Especially when I read about these Ketu, Venus and Mercury planets all being in Leo, too; I found myself deeply relating to these more negative descriptions of Leo!

#6 – My Mars planet too was supposed to be much more negative in my chart due to being in Mars' chief, negative Sign of #4 Cancer. In fact, Mars is said to be worst or "debilitated" when found in this Sign. So I then read about Mars full positive vs. negative traits. And it was at this time that I discovered that this important Mars part of my chart, was also so very negative. I was most definitely living more of the passive and timid side of one such negative Mars-planet when Mars is found in this least positive Sign of Cancer.

#7 – The final negative planet I found in my chart was that unique Rahu planet which I then examined in terms of being within that unique #11 Sign of Aquarius as well as being within the specific 5th House in my chart. For here, the negative quality I related to the most here was in terms of Rahu's negative effects upon my 5th House love life! When I read about how the 5th House was also supposed to be related to one's pre-marital life and love and romance, I began to better understand why I had so long had an almost crazy, love-addiction! For years however, I just thought that I was a kind of romantic guy.

Now, I began to realize that my Rahu-planet here was actually more symbolic of having such unique Rahu addictive and obsessive tendencies. And, since my Rahu was in this 5th House of love and romance I began to now, better understand that I did in fact, have such obsessive romantic tendencies.

I too often felt that if I didn't have that most wonderful, soul-mate in my life; that my life would have no meaning or happiness.

Conclusion – Though, it can of course be quite disappointing and frustrating to find so many negatives within both one's chart or inner life. Still because I was now so very committed to trying and finding ways in which one might be able to improve one's especially negative planets; I then discovered this greatest of self-development strategies. Which is how these very same negative planetary configurations themselves, also contains that exact new knowledge and wisdom which is needed, in our lives!

For example, take any of these so-called many negative planets but now look slightly differently at these same negative planetary configurations.

#1 – Take that so very negative Moon planet for example. I not only found out how these unique details of my Moon were responsible for all of my many, mental and emotional frustrations in my life but I then began to learn how these very same, so-called negative configurations, were also so very deeply representative of that new, Moon knowledge and wisdom that I so very needed in my life!

The fact that I'd been born with one such very tiny and small Moon of sunlight when I was born, then led me to discovering important and profound ways in which I could literally increase that degree of Sunlight for my Moon. The two chief ways that I discovered one could profoundly strengthen one's interior Moon-nature were 1) meditating and 2) paying closer attention to these regular, monthly Moon cycles.

You probably already know that the Moon waxes and wanes each month. We know of this as the Full Moon and nil Moon times. However, most people don't realize how beneficial it is to pay closer attention to these two, unique Moon cycles. When I learned this, that I could benefit by learning how to 'rest' more when the Moon is found waning and then, 'doing more' when the Moon is found getting bigger, I found a much unexpected benefit! Not only did I find myself getting along better with life, itself. But, I found that my own, interior Moon nature immediately became stronger and more full and more steady and positive in my life!

Another unique way in which I found my supposedly more negative Moon situation could also help me to improve my very Moon-nature, was in terms of that unique Sign that my Moon had been in. Though when I initially read about what the Moon in Virgo might tend to be about; I right away discovered that I'd been living very much, more of the negative side of Virgo!

For as long as I could remember, I was very Moon-Virgo self-critical and way too hard on myself as well as being very fault finding, fastidious and perfectionist oriented! And this is why it is often said that such a Moon in Virgo situation is in fact, one of one's chief, negative planets.

Now, however that I was beginning to explore 'how' I might be able to improve all such negative planets within my chart, I then discovered the most surprising and extraordinary ways in which this "Virgo" part of ourselves can also be improved!

162

Looking backward now I see how two rather innocent Virgo experiences helped me to discover 'how' Virgo is meant to be improved. For example, when I was in high school I had a conversation with my mother one time, that ended up being extremely revealing.

I'd been having some difficulties with a class writing assignment and I asked her for some help. She listened quietly to why I was having the problem that I was having. And, then she simply said: "You know Mark, it doesn't have to be so very, perfect."

Since, neither of us knew anything about astrology at this time I didn't take this as any kind of astrological observation.

But, now looking backward, I see how something profound and significant did in fact, shift inside of me from this one, mother suggestion! I suddenly did stop sensing that everything had to be so very perfect.

Later, I would hear another such Virgo self-development expression. This time it was many years later and I was listening to another of the Maharishi's many video tape lectures. This time he was talking about yoga philosophy and he then said:

"We shouldn't seek perfection in the relative, (or world), it does not exist. Instead seek perfection inside, in that unbounded field of pure awareness which alone is perfect!"

Now, I began to understand Virgo much more clearly. Like all such Signs, Virgo too has both a positive and negative side. Though, most of the time, only more of the negative side of Virgo is well-understood. And, for such individuals being born with any and all such Virgo-planets, many more of these negative expressions of Virgo will be found.

Being very overly self-critical, seeing the faults of others, being so very critical, too fastidious, too anal in this obsessive, compulsive way, … (ever see the TV show Monk! He was most definitely one such Virgo, impaired individual. And when I did the unique astrological chart of that actor Tony Shalhoub who played so very well, such an obsessive personality; as it turned out in real life he too had been born with such a unique Sun in Virgo nature!)

Now, I began to understand. If you are able to find that true "perfection" that only exists inside, in the spiritual, in that inherent oneness with almighty God, who alone is truly perfect; than you can begin to let go of that relative habit of wishing to be so perfect, on the outside!

And that's what I did. Since, I in fact, had two such personal Virgo planets, both my Moon and Saturn, I now began to focus on finding true perfection inside, in that unbounded field of pure consciousness which can in fact be located at the very source of thought, during meditation.

Then, I also made a point of letting go of my previous habit of being so Virgo anal, on the outside and even internally, within my very self. And, both of these activities then helped me to grow within my very real, Virgo part of me than ever before!

I also began exploring that other main aspect of my Moon planet which was that I was also supposed to have been born with such a negative Moon due to being born in one such more negative 12th House. This 12th House is often called the House of Loss and those who get born with personal planets here will find that they are born at 'loss' to those very planets.

I now learned how I had been born at loss with my Moon here. I now began to explore however, how I might better grow within this unique quality of Moon-find! And I did this innocently just by studying the Moon's very nature and what it was supposed to be all about. I also studied how changeable it was in its constantly waxing and waning modes, each month.

I even explored how the Moon was indeed such an innocent symbol of the human mind and those born with their Moon's in different Signs would end up having such different, human mental natures.

I also discovered at this point that this Moon part of us represents how caring, compassionate and motherly we will be in our lives. Then, it occurred to me, perhaps I can increase my Moon part of me by consciously choosing to be more caring, compassionate and motherly.

Moon Conclusion - And, that's what I did and from all of these Moon self-development ways, I then found out just how much more positive and auspicious my Moon planet could become. I then over time, learned these very same things about each of my other negative planets as well.

#2 - My Negative Saturn – I also learned that my Saturn in Virgo could also be improved from becoming more in-tune with that much more positive side of Virgo. Also, that symbolism of being in the 12th House helped me to realize that as I studied and became more knowledgeable about Saturn, itself, this would very profoundly improve my own, Saturn nature.

This Saturn planet too has both a positive and negative side and as one studies this one will first, discover just how much of that negative side one is in fact, living. And, then you can make a conscious choice to embrace and grow within more of the positive side of Saturn which will then most profoundly help one to grow and improve one's very Saturn nature.

Saturn Positive – Conclusion – I now discovered how those very same, so-called negative aspects of my Saturn planet also contained that very same, new Saturn knowledge and wisdom which I so very needed in my very life!

#3, 4 & 5 – My Many Negative Leo Planets - I then discovered how there was much new Leo knowledge and wisdom to be found within those so-called more negative Mercury and Venus planets which previously had only been understood in terms of being more indicative of such negative, bad habits as being very selfish and self-centered.

As I then explored ways in which I could literally step into a much more giving and selfless part of myself, I found these previously negative Venus and Mercury planets, helped me to see, exactly how and where I was supposed to grow and become much less self-centered.

#6 – My Negative Mars Planet – My uniquely negative Mars in Cancer placement was found to be particularly fascinating as I now began to explore how I might improve this part of myself. For example, Cancer represents how we care and give and when certain planets are found in Cancer, (like Mars) then one can have the bad habit of over-giving!

I then learned how to give less, in such an imbalanced way and after a while I began to see how this uniquely more negative Mars in Cancer part of me, literally helped me to step into a much more positive Mars vibration.

#7 – My Last Negative Rahu Planet – Also helped me to find those unique Rahu improvements which were so necessary in my life. I discovered first how Rahu in one's 5th House can be so very indicative of such addictive, romantic entanglements. And, as I learned to be less obsessive about my love life and romantic interests I found out exactly how I could be improving this Rahu part of my inner life.

Conclusion – Examine any of your so-called most negative planets but not discover how these very same negative configurations also contain that exact new knowledge and wisdom that you so very need, in this life! And you too will discover this most exciting way in which you can improve any and all of your personal planets.

CHAPTER 7

EMBRACING EXALTED PLANETS!

"Discover those unique times in which each of these Planets will be found moving through their best and most favorable of exalted Signs. And then embrace these!"

~ Mark Kincaid

Looking back now too, I see that one of the absolutely most profound of such self-development techniques that I found myself stumbling into, was this unique one which is called: "embracing one's exalted planets!"

Even within traditional astrology, there has long been this idea of positive and negative planets. In other words, the very rules and principles of astrology that are there to classify which of our personal planets will be found positive or negative for us! In my own chart, this most simple of ideas helped me to see why I did have at least two positive planets even while I also had so many other, more negative ones.

Every planet then is said to have some Signs which represent when these very same parts of ourselves will be more well developed and positive while other such planetary-Signs will then be more indicative of the our more negative human habits and dysfunctional aspects of ourselves.

The Planet's Exalted Signs - The Moon for example is said to be best or most positive and auspicious when found within it's exalted #2 Sign of Taurus! The Sun part of us is said to be exalted or the most positive and favorable when found within the unique, #1 Sign of Aries.

And those individuals who do in fact, get born with such exalted Moon and Sun planets will then be those very individuals who find themselves living many more of the most positive aspects of these planets.

We had a sister Beth who'd been born under one such exalted Moon in Taurus nature and a brother, who'd been born with an exalted Sun-planets. In both of these ways, each of these siblings of mine helped me to see just what such a rarefied and positive planetary Sign-position could be all about.

Then, as it turns out, there are unique times of each month and year when these same Moon and Sun planets will be found moving through these best of exalted Signs.

The Moon for example, is exalted every month when found moving through that unique #2 Sign of Taurus. The Sun's exaltation occurs every year from about the 15th of the month of April to about the 15th of May.

Then there is that other important Mercury planet which also has its exalted status when found moving through that unique #6 Sign of Virgo.

Mars too has an exalted #10 Sign of Capricorn and every year, both Mercury and Mars will be found at some point, to be in fact, moving through their best of exalted Signs.

Even Saturn and Jupiter planets have such most positive and favorably auspicious, exalted Signs. Though, because they move very slowly their exalted Signs will not happen each year. Saturn is exalted in that unique #7 Sign of Libra while Jupiter is exalted in that very different, #4 Sign of Cancer.

Conclusion – Pay closer attention to these unique times when each of these natural planets of astrology are exalted, both within the world and out there and within those family members and friends and then as you learn how to 'embrace' these exalted opportunities, more you'll find yourself literally growing and becoming more exalted within your very self!

For example, we can now see which days ahead will find the Moon moving through its best of Signs.

The Moon's Exaltation in #2 Taurus – As you can see in this chart included on the next page her, on this day of July 12th of 2015, the Moon was in fact found moving through its exalted #2 Sign of Taurus on this day.

In fact, the Moon is found exalted for 2 ½ days each month and when you focus more on these days, you too will have the most delicious of experience as to just what such a more highly evolved, Moon really feels like.

In 2016 for example, pay closer attention to these exalted Moon times:

January 19th & 20th,
February 15th & 16th,
March 13th & 14th,
April 10th & 11th,
May 7th & 8th, and
June 4th & 5th.

Notice too how these days do not occur on the same days of each month because there is the Moon cycle is a 28-day one while the typical Sun-cycle that our calendars are based on are a 30-day cycle.

Also, pay just as much attention to when the Moon is found waxing and the most big and bright from its ½ Full to completely Full status. And, finally when the Moon is found moving through its second best Sign of #4 Cancer, these days too will help you to become more well-developed and even much more positive within your inherent Moon-nature!

Birth Chart

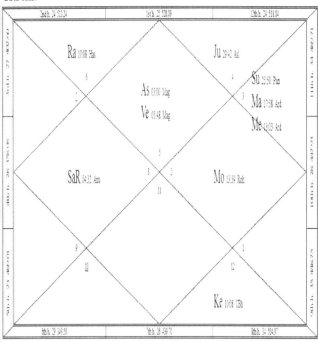

[1 of 9] You are looking at the first of the 300 available worksheets. Worksheets are highly customizable, interactive screens. There are three areas within the worksheet: the title bar at the top, the workspace in the middle, and this help area at the bottom. >>

PREV NEX

170

The Sun's Exaltation In #1 – Aries - Then there is the Sun's best of exalted Signs when it is found moving into and through the complete Sign of #1 Aries for 30 days every year, between the middle of April to the middle of May.

I personally got the most out of these days because I wanted to become ever stronger and more powerful within my very Sun-nature because I knew that one's basic Sun, self-confidence and self-worth was extremely important for all that one wants to achieve and accomplish in one's life.

This chart is made for one such April 14th of 2016 which will then begin the Sun's next exalted 30-days. I gained the most increase of such positive Sun-vibrations for myself by just paying the closest attention to these whole months when the Sun is found moving through its most positive and auspicious of Signs.

The Sun's exalted days over the next few years will begin on:

April 14th of 2016 –
April 14th of 2017, to
April 14th of 2018 and on and on.

Pay just as much attention to the Sun's second best of Sign movements when it spends 30 days moving through that unique #5 Sign of Leo which it does every year from about the 14th of August to the 12th of September!

And finally, find those personal friends and family members who also got born with such exalted Sun's and Sun's in Leo, and each of these individuals will also help you to more deeply understand just how powerful and favorable the Sun can be within your self!

Birth Chart

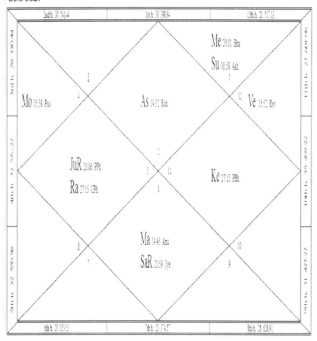

[1 of 9] You are looking at the first of the 300 available worksheets. Worksheets are highly customizable, interactive screens. There are three areas within the worksheet: the title bar at the top, the workspace in the middle, and this help area at the bottom. >>

PREV NEXT

172

Venus – Exaltation in #12 Pisces – Then there is that unique time of each year, when this all-important, giving, loving and appreciative Venus planet is found moving through its best of exalted Signs of #12 Pisces.

Take this next year's exalted Venus time starting from April 1st of 2016! And Venus remains in exalted #12 Pisces until the 24th.

Because most people do not get naturally born with such most favorable and auspicious of Venus planets, such exalted Venus times can go a long way in terms of helping us to discover just what such an exalted, "unconditionally loving" Venus, feels like! I have also experienced 25 times now, over these last twenty-five years and each of these uniquely most wonderful of Venus times have helped me to grow and self-improve within my own, unique Venus nature.

January 27, 2017 – And remains in exalted #12 Pisces until May 30th! This year's exalted Venus time is even longer because during this time, Venus also goes retrograde for a number of weeks.

Also, pay closer attention to the two, next most positive, Venus Signs which are the "Own Signs" of Venus. Venus is very happy and positive when found in #2 Taurus and #7 Libra. This next, year, notice that Venus is found in these positive Signs during these dates:

Venus in #2 Taurus – May 20th – June 12th – 2016 and
Venus in #7 Libra – From Sept. 19th – Oct. 12th – 2016

Pay also the most attention to those friends and family members who also got born under either this Venus in exalted Pisces nature or Venus in either #2 Taurus or Libra. And, you will find such delicious and surprising Venus self-growth happening within your very self. Regardless as to how positive

Of a Venus nature, you originally started out with.

Prashna Apr 1, 2016 05:43:09   < 1. Birth chart ▷

Birth Chart

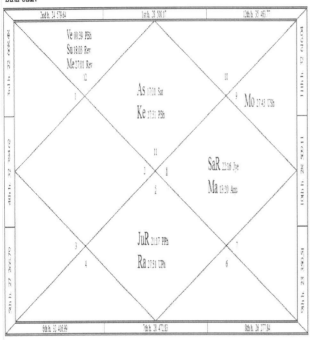

[1 of 9] You are looking at the first of the 300 available worksheets. Worksheets are highly customizable, interactive screens. There are three areas within the worksheet: the title bar at the top, the workspace in the middle, and this help area at the bottom. >>

PREV NEXT

174

Mars – Exaltation – Times – Then there will be those unique times of each year, when this very different of Mars planets will be found moving through its unique, exalted, #10 Sign of Capricorn. This next year, for example, that Mars or "Ma" planet will be found moving into this specific #10 Sign of Capricorn starting on November 1st of 2016.

Because Mars moves slightly slower than either the Sun, Venus or other planets it will be found moving more slowly through these unique 12 Signs of the astrology. In fact, the last time Mars was found 'exalted' or moving through its best of Signs in #10 Capricorn, it was in November of 2014. This next exalted Mars time starting on November 1st of 2016 then will last till the 11th of December.

What I've found particularly significant about Mars' 'exalted' days is just what a great contrast such positive Mars times are, compared with those many other Signs-times, which tend to be much less, positive!

Mars will next be found exalted starting on May 2nd of 2018!

Though, of course, there are two other great Mars Signs of #1 Aries and #8 Scorpio which are Mars' two chief, Own Signs. All three of these most positive of Mars times will go a long way in terms of presenting to you exactly what such a positive and favorable Mars nature can be like.

And, of course, continue to search out and find those friends or family members who also got born with such more well-developed, personal Mars natures. Our mother got born with one such exalted Mars-nature and from the moment I realized this about her, I was able to discover just how she was such a great Mars, role-model for me!

Even other friends of 'stars' can be found to have such unique Mars-natures. Oprah for example got born with her Mars in that second, very positive, Mars in #8 Scorpio nature and she

Has been without a doubt such a Mars champion in her life

Birth Chart

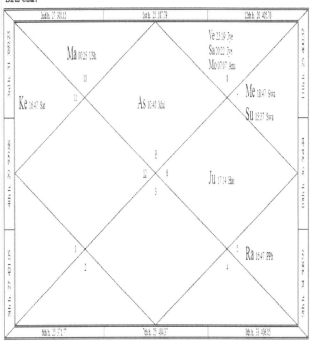

[1 of 9] You are looking at the first of the 300 available worksheets. Worksheets are highly customizable, interactive screens. There are three areas within the worksheet: the title bar at the top, the workspace in the middle, and this help area at the bottom. »

PREV NEXT

Mercury's – Exalted – in #6 Virgo – Then there is that equally as important Mercury planet which represents how 'well' we will think, choose, decide and discriminate. When Mercury is found moving through this unique #6 Sign of Virgo, not only will Mercury be found flowing in this most uplifting, positive and 'exalted' ways; but these same kinds of Mercury times will also serve as great tools and examples as to just how on can powerfully self-improve one's own, personal Mercury-nature.

The very next time Mercury will be found 'exalted' will be August 23rd of 2015. And, then after that Mercury will next be found 'exalted' again starting on August 19th of 2016! As you can see, Mercury's movement is almost as regular as the Sun's. Though, Mercury this next year will also be found quickly moving into its retrograde or "R" time which will suddenly catapult Mercury backward in terms of these exact degrees of that Sign where Mercury is also moving through.

This year then will quite extend Mercury's "general" 4-5 weeks of exalted days, suddenly into even more such auspicious Mercury times. Mercury's next exalted time will then find Mercury even going all the way backward and even into the previous, #5 Sign of Leo. Finally, Mercury's next retrograde motion will end on the 31st of August of 2016 which means it will suddenly be found moving ahead again.

Mercury's next exaltation - starting on October 4th of 2016.

Mercury's so-called exalted times will be particularly auspicious because most people can benefit by discovering how to so significantly self-improve and literally self-develop one's all-important Mercury, decision making abilities.

Pay closer attention to that other positive Mercury time when found flowing through #3 Gemini which is Mercury's Own Sign. Pay such closer attention to all these unique times and those friends and family members who also got born with such more well-developed Mercury-natures and all of these will

Help one to grow more fully within one's very Mercury-nature.

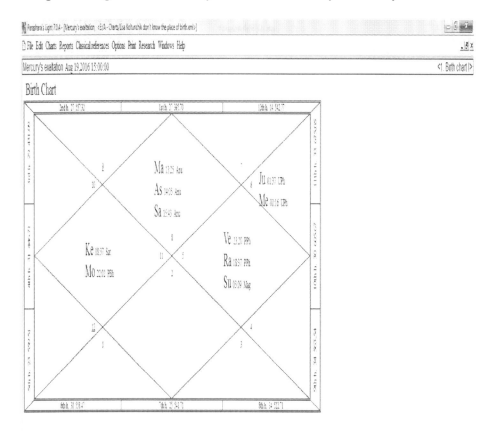

The last two planets worth considering will be Jupiter and Saturn. Though because they move so much more slowly than all of the other planets, their exalted Signs will only occur much less frequently. Jupiter is exalted for a year, only every 12 years while Saturn's exaltation only occurs every 30 years!

Jupiter's Exalted – Times – Jupiter's last exalted time in this very unique #4 Cancer first began in early July of 2002. I had by now been watching these daily Transits each day since 1989 or for about twelve years by this point. I had also begun experiencing these most wondrous and surprising, 'exalted' times for a number of years but never before, had I experienced Jupiter's best of positive, vibrations.

I had also learned at this point how to find those unique Houses within one's chart 'where' these very same Transits will be found flowing. Since, Jupiter's exaltation is supposed to be found flowing through #4 Cancer and I'd also learned how in my chart, this same Cancer was in my 10th House of career; I then watched to see how this unique Jupiter might be affecting me and my career-life. Right away almost the very day, Jupiter first moved into Cancer I felt that very auspicious and beneficial, even holy guru vibration now flowing to me and into my career-life.

12 years later as Jupiter was about to be found moving into #4 Cancer again, I was now even much more well-prepared and experienced in taking such greatest advantage of these planet's best of Signs-vibrations. From that very first day of July 19th of 2014, that Jupiter first moved into exalted, #4 Cancer I was again, so very appreciative that I'd been led to discovering these unique times when the guru of the universe would be found flowing in its best of Signs.

I felt more the hand of God moving through me at this time and the next 12 months of Jupiter's exalted days, were some of my happiest and most accomplished ever. I in fact, wrote and published four new Nature's Astrology books at this time which I'd been thinking about for years! Now, looking ahead, let's find those next two years when Jupiter will be next, moving through its Own Signs of #9 Sagittarius and #12 Pisces.

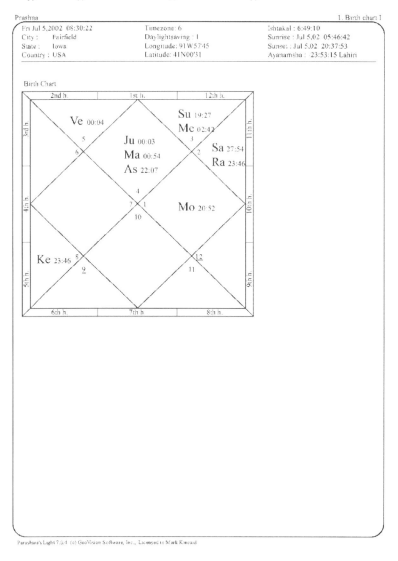

Parashara's Light 7.0.4 (c) GeoVision Software, Inc., Licensed to Mark Kincaid

For example, Jupiter next moves into Sagittarius on Nov. 5th of 2019 and will remain there for a whole year! Jupiter's next, #12 Pisces Transit will then begin on April 13th of 2022. Of course also pay such close attention to those unique friends, family members and individuals who also got born with such auspicious and positive Jupiter-planets. When I discovered that my mother too had that very wonderful Jupiter in #12 Pisces in her chart that helped me to much more deeply appreciate how very spiritual she was. And, most recently I discovered how that very famous new teacher Donald Neale Walsh, author of the landmark book: "Conversations of God" had also been born with such an auspicious, exalted Jupiter in Cancer within his own, personal chart.

Saturn's Exaltation – in #7 Libra – I then began realize that Saturn too had an exalted Sign. Though, because it moves so very slowly, it would only be found moving into Libra, every 30 years! Fortunately, one such exalted Saturn time was about to happen for us, first starting on Nov. 15th of 2011. Though, I'd never experienced this before, since the last time, 30 years earlier, I'd not even been studying astrology in 1981!

Though because I'd now been watching Saturn at least moving through all of its other Signs, I at least now knew what these most negative Signs of Cancer were all about.

From that very first day in November of 2011 that Jupiter first stepped into Libra, I felt a divine, heavenly cherub had descended to this earth. Suddenly, Saturn was all smiles and only more of the positive side of Saturn were found manifesting at this time.

And, because Saturn's exalted times will last for 2 ½ years, I found myself most deeply embracing Saturn during these times and now looking backward realize, I had now had one of the greatest, astrological experiences of my life.

During much of this previous time, I felt that very silent, still and powerfully balanced, most positive potential of Saturn manifesting during these times and as a result of watching these, I found my own, personal Saturn nature, becoming more positive than I would have ever thought possible.

Of course also find those unique individuals within your family and friend-circles who also got born with such positive and auspicious of Saturn's. One of my sisters and close friends of mine both had been born with such a most positive and uplifting of Saturn-natures and those years now that I've watched them and then eventually realized: "Hey, I could be more like that!" ... I realized just how such an exalted Saturn is in fact, possible to be more greatly embraced.

I even wrote on, finished and published my definite Saturn book called "Saturn is Shiva" during that most recent exalted Saturn time.

The two other, more positive Own Signs of Saturn coming up with be first starting on January 24th of 2020 when Saturn first moves into that next, #10 Sign of Capricorn. For all of the next 2 ½ years Saturn will then be found moving in such a much more positive and favorable of ways. And, Saturn will be found moving into its next Own Sign of #11 Aquarius first starting January 18th of 2023. So, be sure to catch these most wonderful times because most everyone can benefit by discovering how to create such a better Saturn-reality within themselves.

Conclusion – Each of these very short and quick Moon exalted times and very lengthy, month-long Sun-exalted times will do more for helping one to grow and self-progress than anything else. I now, looking back over 25 years of this exalted searching have gained more insights and practical examples as just what these planet's highest of vibrations can be like.

And every month and year that I experienced these for myself I found these very same, all-important planetary parts of my human nature, continuing to grow and become more and more positive than I would have ever thought possible.

Be sure not to miss a single exalted day in all of this next, year of 2016, 2017 or 2018... whenever you hear about this most wonderful exalted, planetary possibilities!

CHAPTER 8

ASTROLOGY – THE SCIENCE OF HUMAN SUCCESS!

"You have to learn the rules of the game. And, then you have to play better than anyone else."

~ Albert Einstein

As if these weren't even enough reasons to pay closer attention to one's astrology; then there is that equally as profound way in which we can use our charts to become more "successful", in our lives!

So far, even traditional astrology has long had this unique idea and concept of one's Positive vs. Negative planets. Simply understood, where we each have our positive and negative planets will define exactly 'where' we're each already experiencing the most natural success as well as where we're struggling and experiencing all of our human frustrations.

Take this traditional astrological idea of the "Houses" for example. These define the literal areas of the life in which we will find ourselves being either successful or struggling! These Houses of astrology as we briefly discussed in that initial chapter on our eastern charts, has long been known to be very indicative of those unique areas of the life which we're already interested in.

The Astrological Houses

For instance, there is that so-called 10th House of astrology which is typically called one's 10th House of career. And depending on whether one gets born with either positive or negative, personal planets 'here', this will determine whether or not one will achieve career success or struggle and fail in one's career!

In fact, all of the natural rules and principles of astrology have been there to determine this quality of positive vs. negative planets which in turn, determines where we're going to have ease and natural fulfillment of desire or struggle and find human disappointments!

Since, this has long been one of the most important of all natural, astrological ideas or concepts, this has helped millions of people to better understand their very lives.

Though, since very little was understood in terms of 'how' we are also capable of dramatically self-improving or self-developing our same, negative planets; most people were not able to discover then how to become more successful in their lives, until now!

Today, because much more is being discovered as to how we can powerfully self-improve and self-develop our especially most negative and dysfunctional of personal planets; we now have that so very important ability to create greater success in our very lives.

One day, one of my students came to me and had just finished reading one of the Nature's Astrology newsletters that I had written about this very same idea of positive and negative planets and success and failure.

She wanted to then to know which of her own personal planets were her positive vs. negative planets and how she might be able to experience even greater success by learning how to significantly improve and self-develop those very same, most negative of personal planets.

She then said this: "Mark, I have been reading about your take on astrology now for a while. And, yet today, I think I finally got what you've long been saying. I am now ready to come to understand within my own chart, 'why' I am the way that I am and most importantly how I might be able to achieve greater success in my life."

When I then asked her which 'areas' of her life she was the most interested in, she had this to say: "Let's see. I'd have to say I've long felt like I had big goals. I've also seemed to have some kind of clarity as to what I've always wanted. I've unfortunately also felt held back and delayed from achieving what I've wanted." I then asked her: "And, which specific areas of your life do you find to be the most disappointing?"

She then said: "I'd have to say in terms of my work or career and also in terms of making money and my health. Sometimes I find all kinds of health complaints coming when I'm just trying to achieve greater success in my life!"

I then told her why I so love hearing people's exact words when they're expressing themselves. Because one can hear very clearly, these unique aspects of one's personal chart, speaking, when we talk! So, when she said she had "big goals" and "big aspirations" that made me think of her 11th House! As you can

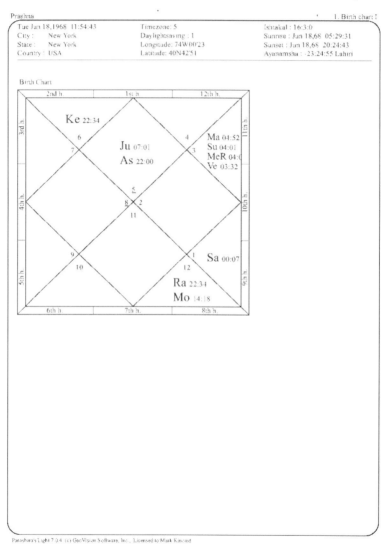

Parashara's Light 7.0.4 (c) GeoVision Software, Inc., Licensed to Mark Kincaid

see here in her chart, she has in fact, most of her planets in this same, 11th House of one's life goals, dreams and aspirations. The 11th House is quite often called the House of financial gain but it also represents just as important human goals and desires and aspirations. I then said: "See how you've got your Sun, Mars, Mercury and Venus planets all in this same House? This means the kind of person who would be so intensely interested in achieving their life's goals and dreams."

She then asked: "And can you tell me why I also feel so held back from my very same desires and goals?" I then said: "Absolutely, and that is due to your personal Saturn planet which is by the way, 'why' we feel held back, restricted and impatient in our lives. And, your Saturn is that "Sa" here within your so-called 9th House which is indicative of having been born with one more negative kind of Saturn planets. And from this position, this very same Saturn part of you is directly aspecting and therefore influencing your same, 11th House due to Saturn's 3rd House Aspect Away.

In other words, your personal chart, not only fits you and we can easily find now where you have your most important positive and negative planets. Because where you have your so-called more positive planets this is why you're able to already experience some degree of natural success while at the same time, where you have your so-called more negative planets; represents where you're going to be found struggling and even experiencing your greatest human difficulties and frustrations.

I also loved hearing your exact words because when you said you've had big goals I found this so very helpful because this confirmed for me how this 11th House part of your chart, really does fit you! And, when you said that you also had some, greater "clarity" that made me think of the unique Mercury-planet which in fact, that part of us which will bring either natural clarity of mind or intellectual confusion!

And you can see this as your Mercury which was born in what

is traditionally called the "Own Sign" of Mercury which is that very same, #3 Sign of Gemini. This almost always means the kind of person who will get born with such, a more well-developed and positive intellectual part of your human nature.

She then asked again: "Tell me some more about why Saturn means that delaying and being held back, kind of quality." I then said: "Saturn's very unique nature is to express to us, just how in-tune we are with ourselves and the universe. Though, sometimes Saturn's very real influences will be of a more positive kind. Most of the time however, for most people; Saturn is quite often more indicative of one of their less than positive, human tendencies.

We live in such a world today that is hugely out of balance and stressed out even. So, it's not surprising that you are finding yourself experiencing more of this negative side of Saturn. Though, what this still means that you're supposed to also learn how to improve and step into an even more positive side of your Saturn planet. And when you do this much of those more negative qualities of Saturn will then begin to disappear!"

She then asked: "And, is there anything that I can do to change this?" I then said: "Historically, most of traditional astrology from both the west and east has not been able to 'teach' people as to how they might change or improve our lives by learning how to change and improve our especially most negative of personal planets.

But, now that more of this most important natural self-improvement capability is beginning to be better understood, astrology is going to be quickly understood as the most important of success tools, in this life!"

She then asked: "Can you go into more detail as to how I might be able to improve my, eh, Saturn planet then?" I then said: "Yes, and in fact since I've spent most of my last 28 years exploring this new astrological breakthrough and how we can powerfully improve and self-develop ourselves by changing and improving our natural planets; I have accumulated more new information and wisdom in this regard, than ever before.

For example, most other people also find themselves experiencing the most frustrations and difficulties due to having been born with one such, most negative of personal Saturn planets. Therefore, my very second most important book I wrote was a book devoted completely to Saturn which then became known as that new book: "Saturn is Shiva". This book in fact, has more Saturn remedies and remedial measures for Saturn improvement than any previous astrological book ever written. So, in addition to what we're talking about today, I recommend that you also take advantage of this new book since your own personal Saturn planet is one of your most important of negative planets."

We of course spent quite a bit of time at least covering some of the most important ways in which you could most powerfully improve this very same Saturn part of herself. I then said: "It will be helpful for you to understand how there are both Holistic and Specific ways in which you can improve all such planets. For example, there are some techniques and practices that will be holistic in their very nature and 'everyone' can benefit from these more holistic solutions.

The chief holistic solutions for Saturn are 1) meditating because meditation, literally enlivens a greater calmness and silent stillness within us which will then dramatically improve this Saturn part of us. 2) – Secondly, there is another holistic Saturn practice which I like to call, simply "resting" more! Because what do doctors universally say to their patients? Regardless as to what dis-ease or disease they are experiencing they are told: "Go home, take these prescriptions and get plenty of rest!"

As it turns out Rest is the universal formula for all that ails and frustrates us and I've found in most people that they can receive tremendous benefits by simply taking one or two more hours of rest, each evening." She then asked: "If it is this simple, how come so many still have so many eh, Saturn problems in their lives?" I then said: "It is because we still live in one such, most negative Saturn-age! In other words, we still live in such a human time and culture that values more deeply, being active and outward. We don't value the down times of life. We hate having to go home and rest and be quiet! We'd much rather be more outward, busy and active and as a result, much of our innate Saturn needs are quite often neglected or ignored!

This then leads to what I consider to be a third, just as important, Saturn, holistic solution. This is then to make a point of studying and coming to appreciate this inherent value and profundity of such Saturn rest, significance more, now!

For example when I first learned to meditate, at the same time I was learning to meditate, many of the lectures and videos I watched included discussions as to this great value and profundity of rest in life. Some of the most fascinating ideas or expressions I heard, included these:

"Rest is the basis of activity!" - This one idea alone had the most powerful and immediate of positive influences upon me. Because I too had been born with one such most negative of personal Saturn planets, I too needed to understand this deep principle of rest more profoundly. In fact, from the very moment that I heard this most simple of ideas, I saw just how much I didn't like resting. I didn't like going to bed early and I didn't like taking the time necessary to rest more!

But, now I had at least a new idea that right away began to change my previous notions and understanding. And as I continued studying and appreciating this deepest value of 'rest' principles more profoundly, I found myself becoming much changed and even improved within my own, internal Saturn part of myself.

She then asked: "Were there any other Saturn ideas you also

liked?" I then said: "Yes, there were two others that I especially enjoyed. This one: "How well we rest the day before will have a lot to do with how successful our next day will be." And, another that I also liked was this one: "Do less and accomplish more!"

Though, initially that felt so very strange and even counter intuitive to me even though I was now meditating and right away beginning to feel much better simply by meditating more."

She then said: "I sense how helpful this might be, but I have to admit that I've always been a kind of work alcoholic and felt better about myself if I was working hard!" I then said: "This then also leads me to discuss some of those other most unique "specific" kinds of Saturn solutions which will be particularly advantageous for you, personally!

For example, the exact Sign and House that our personal Saturn's are in will then describe the unique ways in which we're each meant to significantly self-improve and self-develop our own, personal Saturn planets. I got born with my Saturn more negatively positioned within my 12th House of Loss, in my chart and I found this particular detail to be particularly meaningful and significant for me, personally."

She then asked: "And, my own Saturn then?" I then said: "In your case, your Saturn in the 9th House also has one such unique meaning while that other Sign placement, in that very special, #1 Sign of Aries also has an equally as important meaning and significance for you, personally."

We then went into much more detail about these two main aspects of her personal Saturn, planet. I said things like this too: "The chief meaning for your Saturn here is that it is in that very unique #1 Sign of Aries which as it turns out is Saturn's least positive and most negative of Signs. Saturn is even called being debilitated or more negative when found in this #1 Sign.

This means the kind of person who got born with a much more busy kind of human nature and not so appreciative of the rest side of life and the importance of resting more!" She then asked: "So, is there anything that I can do to improve this?" I then said: "Yes. In fact, everything that we've been talking about today will now profoundly change you! You will find from this very moment that your own, personal Saturn part of you, begins to change now, just because you are even now, waking up to this deeper, Saturn appreciation."

She then asked: "Anything else that you feel to say about my Saturn?" I then said: "Because your Saturn is directly found flowing into your 11th House due to its 3rd Sign and House Aspect Away, one other solution for you will be for you to literally, practice being more patient in your life!" She then said: "I don't know if this will work because I've often felt that I was impatient and could benefit by being more patient but I never figured out how to do this."

I then said: "Now, however, that you're beginning to appreciate more deeply, this all-importance of resting more, you will be sufficiently changed inside enough so that even just choosing to be more patient will be more easy and profound for you, now!"

Though, I knew she didn't realize yet how this could be for here, I knew that if she simply followed even a fit of these most natural Saturn solutions, that she would right away find much Saturn and life improvement for herself.

And, that's exactly what happened. Over the next few weeks and months as we continued to talk and she continued to explore and discover such unique Saturn solutions for herself, she found herself profoundly changing and growing inside and as a result of these most simple Saturn improvements, she began to feel that her natural 11th House goals and aspirations were able to be more easily fulfilled, now.

Though I'd also like to include here one more discussion about her unique "success" reading which included her 11th House itself. I knew for example, that only one or two planets tend to be the most positive in the unique Signs and Houses in which they are found deposited. This means that at least two of her unique planets here within her 11th House might also be more negative and malefic creating!

We first talked about how each Sign has at least one planet which is especially helpful in that very same Sign. There is this natural concept of astrology's which is called Planets in their Own Signs. Every Sign has one planet that is called the natural Lord or ruler of that Sign and for this #3 Sign of Gemini, Mercury is that very same, natural Lord of this Sign.

The fact that she has her Gemini-Ruler planet here within her Gemini Sign then tends to represent that kind of person who will get born with more of the positive side of Mercury and that's why she often felt like she did have such a natural, greater intellectual "clarity" in her life.

But, this also means that some of her other planets here, her Sun and especially Mars and Venus planets, by the way; will all tend to be more representative of the negative side of Gemini. We then began exploring this possibility. Though, sometimes, the Sun can represent more of the positive side of Gemini. However, a quick conversation with here was able to determine that she was most definitely experiencing quite a bit of that most negative side of Gemini.

When I told her what this might be like, she then said: "I am most definitely the kind of person who just loves doing way too many things at the same time. And, that is especially true for me, in terms of making money. I seem to constantly have way too many rods in the fire, so to speak."

I then said: "Your exact words then will show us precisely how such details really do fit you. And, at the same, time, your ability to articulate this more negative side of Gemini, most definitely will be another such example in which your personal chart, is in fact, profoundly speaking to you!"

First we discussed both the complete positive and negative sides of Gemini itself. And I said: "The chief positives of Gemini include natural, greater intellectual abilities as well as very good communicative skills and such a greater ability to intellectually, self-understand. We then discussed that equally as important negative side of Gemini which includes that most unique Gemini negative of too often, "doing way too many things at the same time."

We then went into much more detail about her Mars planet here which almost always in Gemini means being too Mars aggressive in this natural tendency to do way too many things at the same time. She then had this to say: "Well, that is most definitely me! I have to agree about this. I so love being not only busy but I literally have loved juggling so many plates at the same time!"

I then said: "And, I believe because of your very good Mercury planet here, sometimes, this will work out for you and you will instead find at least some positive repercussions of this, yes? She then said: "Eh, yes, I think you're right. In fact, quite often at work I am called in when such a demanding schedule or time is needed. When so many especially chaotic things are going on at the same time, I am often chosen to try and bring greater order to such situations."

I then said: "And, this again is due to that better Mercury planet there. Though each of these other planets would also tend to be more representative of this more negative side of Gemini, manifesting in your life, too." She then asked: "And, how do you think this specific situation in my 11th House will affect my 11th House goals and aspirations!"

I also was now marveling at her greater, Mercury planet here operating even bringing to her such a quicker appreciation and understanding about everything that we were talking about.

I then said: "In your case, both your Mars and Venus planets here will make you strive to achieve and accomplish your 11th House goals and aspirations in this more negative and undermining of ways. In other words, you will spontaneously feel to do two, three or even four and then too often, too many things at the same, time! And the effect of this will be that this does diminish your 11th House of financial gain.

The chief solution here then is for you to create a greater calmness and simplicity within your very self and inherent, Gemini nature and one of the other chief ways you will be able to do this will for you to choose to do less, too many things at the same time!

Of course as you are also able to improve your very Saturn nature at the same time, that self-growth there too will also overlap and create within you just such a more vivid, less complicated Gemini vibration within yourself, which then will automatically flow better into your 11th House goals and aspirations!"

Conclusion: And so it will go within everyone else, as well.

Everyone will get born with similar situations though everyone too will find that their essential astrological details are different. Let's now finish this chapter's discussion on "success" by looking into such specific details of another person's individual chart.

This next chart here is the chart of a man who came to me and was having specific, stronger desires to be more successful in their natural career, life. And hearing this I then of course thought of his unique 10th House realities.

And as you can see in this man's chart on the next page here, he had two all-important planets there within his 10th House of career. He had both his Moon, "Mo" and Mars "Ma" planets here and both within that same, #2 Sign of Taurus. Right away too I knew that his Moon would tend to be more indicative of some such positive goings on within his career while his Mars planet here would be more representative of some important tensions and difficulties within his career life.

So, we took it step by step. I've learned first, that every person can benefit deeply by coming to understand what the unique Signs mean when found in those unique Houses or areas of the life that we're interested in. So, we first started talking about what Taurus is all about in his 10th House.

I then said: "This #2 of Taurus here in your 10th House means that you will have a very strong and specific Taurian flavor in terms of how you like to function in career. Where this #2 Taurus is in our charts is quite often where we have a lot of natural love and genuine caring for. And, since your Taurus is here in your career, you might be experiencing this in terms of having a strong love for your career itself, yes?" She then said: "That is amazing that you say this. Because this is most definitely me. I do care very much about my career and I especially care for all that I find myself involved with, at work. But, here's the problem. At the same time that I do care so much, at the same time I also find myself fighting with way too many individuals. So my question is, why does this keep happening to me?

I then said: "This is exactly a good reflection of both of these planets dominating in your 10th House of career. The Moon here brings great positive values and ease and auspicious career experiences. Though, at the same time, this simultaneous Mars planet will bring such different and opposite, fighting qualities and experiences."

She then said: "But, I'm confused. Not only do I have this great feeling of love for my career. But, most of the time I also love that fiery, eh, Marish part of me which makes me very dynamic and intense as well as determined in my career as well." I then said: "Well, this is how astrology works. First, it identifies where we'll be having all of our unique human qualities and tendencies. But, this it makes a value judgment and says, some planets will be positive and favorable, while others will be more negative and very disappointing creating.

This means too that you will tend to have some confusion around this Mars part of you, just because Mars sometimes is so very happy in one's 10th House. But, being in #2 Taurus quite often brings not only tensions and fighting too often, but sometimes even a kind of Taurus rigidity and stubbornness." She then said: "That's fascinating because quite often my associates at work do say that about me, that I am inflexible and rigid. But, I generally think 'they' are the problem."

I then said: "This is exactly my point but the solution then is for you to accept that you do have this wonderful Moon part of yourself and when you're flowing in this more caring and compassionate way, most everything will be fine for you. But, now, the astrological suggestion here is to pull back from some of that intense Marishness. And, instead of just wielding it like a big stick, now begin to explore this possibility, that you just might do better by choosing to refine and tone down, some of this greater Mars-intensity."

In regard to this part of her chart, a few weeks and months later, she came back to me and had this to say: "Mark, I just wanted to tell you how helpful I found our readings. First of all, just knowing these fine distinctions between those two 10th Houses planets of mine helped me to see myself more clearly. And, that suggestion of yours that this Moon part was more positive while my Mars was more negative, helped me immensely!

Even in a few days and couple weeks I found myself, not only feeling better but everyone around me stopped fighting so much and began to appreciate and congratulate me, which still is so very surprising to me." I then said: "You will always have that Mars strength within yourself and still available to you for your career-life. So, you'll be able to use it where necessary and especially if you need to stand up for yourself at times. However, knowing that most of the time, you will do better by toning back that same, Mars energy, just might be one of the best things that you came into this life to learn about yourself."

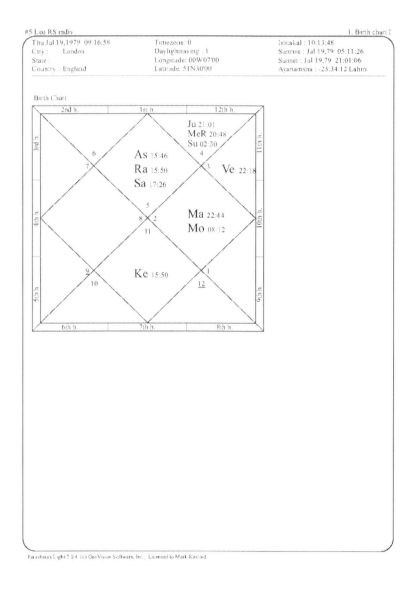

At other times during our readings together, this lady also wanted to focus on her financial concerns. I then told her how one's financial success is such a pure reflection of our 11th and 12th Houses. And, that one's 11th House represents how we will 'gain' financially while our 12th House realities will represent how well we will spend our money. She then said: "Well, I can tell you right away, that I do have a hard time saving money and too often I also have that experience where money just slips through my fingers."

I then said: "Even your very words here too, indicates to me, that this is very likely due to your 12th House. Though we should also talk about those subtle goings on which are happening in your 11th House. Generally, Venus is very happy in your 11th House. Venus is the "Lord" of your 10th House of career, so quite often there will be a close relationship between how you're doing in career and how you're doing with your finances." She then asked: "Isn't this always true?"

I then said: "You might think so. But, what astrology teaches us here is that there can be very different astrological goings on within our career lives, that is not always reflected in similar success within our money Houses. This means then for example, that one could be better in career and less successful in terms of making money. Or one could excel in terms of making money and feel quite a bit of frustration that one isn't necessarily in the right kind of career for oneself."

She then said: "Yes, I'm beginning to understand. So, we can analyze my 11th and 12th Houses in much the same way that we earlier discussed my career-House?" I then said: "That's right and we'll first begin by discussing how these different areas of your chart, will be experienced by you, slightly differently. We too will find both simultaneous positive and negative planetary vibrations going on.

And, like we talked about in your 10th House, we'll make that same recommendation that you can flow more vividly through your better of planets while at the same time, discovering how to refine and slightly change those more negative planets."

She then said: "That sounds very exciting especially since I already found such surprising success in my career life in spite of the fact, that for decades before I never found such improvement at work." We then began discussing the very unique and different energies and natures of those two Signs of #3 Gemini and #4 Cancer. Then we covered what both the positive and negative sides of both of these energies will tend to be like.

She then had this to say: "I really relate to what you're saying about my 11th House. I quite often find myself having many simultaneous goings on at the same time, in terms of trying to make money. And, sometimes I do feel like I'm doing too many things at the same time and don't always have enough energy to take care of so many separate kinds of projects."

I then said: "Not only is this a good expression as to just what #3 Gemini feels like when found within one's 11th House. And, yet at the same time, having your Venus here, can tend to bring out more of the negative side of Gemini, just because Venus is generally thought to not be so very positive when found in Gemini." We then talked about that Lord-planet that rules that same Gemini-energy within his 11th House which is that unique Mercury planet which can be found in that very different 12th House in your chart, in that very different #4 Sign of Cancer.

She then asked: "Didn't you say that such Lord-planets will end up sending back to their Signs-homes, how they are doing?" I then said: "That's absolutely right. So, your 11th House Lord-planet Mercury will end up sending a kind of cosmic 'mail' to its 11th House 'home' just how it is doing, for better or for worse." She then asked: "So, what would you say the primary effect of my Mercury there was all about?"

I then said: "Traditionally, even that historical astrology would say that having one's 11th House Lord-planet in that 12th House of loss would be one negative consequence. And, also having one's Mercury planet itself in that unique #4 Sign of Cancer is also another negative. And, finally, having one's Mercury-planet in that retrograde or "R" motion would be another negative.

Though, what we need to do at this point is to verify this. I'll ask you a few questions here and see if we can discover just how you're experiencing this important Mercury part of you. For example, would you say that too often you find yourself especially confused, maybe even intellectually when you find yourself thinking about your financial goals?" She then said: "Let me think. Eh, now, that you say this, I do sense that you might be right. Quite often I most definitely feel a kind of lack of clarity though of course I never knew why at all." I then said: "This can most definitely be due to your 11th House Lord, Mercury planet being in this more negative situations in your 12th House. This then will mean that there will be some slightly different Mercury suggestions for you."

She then said: "I can hardly wait!" I then said: "Well, first of all, even just focusing on the general techniques of improving Mercury will help your own Mercury-intellect become brighter and less dysfunctional. And yet, there are also important 'specific' solutions which will be particularly helpful as well. For example, one's Mercury intellect-planet is improved by the mental technique and practice of meditating. Meditating literally expands the mind and after meditating, one's whole Moon and Mercury minds will be brighter and clearer.

Though we can also say, that chief specific solution of having one's Mercury in one's 12th House of Loss and in that very unique #4 Sign of Cancer will also bring up other unique ways in which such a Mercury-intellect can be improved. For example, knowing that part of the symbolism of one's 12th House of Loss will be that it will tend to bring up such qualities of loss especially for those unique planets that are in one's 12th House. And, in Mercury's case, the unique solution here is to put more attention on studying what Mercury is all about. How it works, how one's human intellectual side functions and also how you can enliven and strengthen such a uniquely 'dry' and intellectual part of you, which may have been harder since that Moon, emotional part of you has been so very much more positive."

She then asked: "I'm confused. I'm not quite sure what you mean." I then said: "Intellect means logical and cerebral and left-brain which also means associative. 1 + 1 = 2, its logical and makes linear sense. How we feel and how intuitive we are, is most definitely a completely different part of our brain, which you get more easily because of your better functioning Moon."

She then said: "And, making these changes and improvements of both my Venus and Mercury, 11th House planets is going to help me to make more money!?" I then said: "Absolutely. And, sense you already had such a similar experience of success within your 10th House of career, I'm going to bet that you'll do better here as well."

I didn't hear from her after these latest readings for a number of other months. She then did say to me: "Mark, I just wanted to give you some feedback. The first thing I noticed was how your suggestion to pull back from my two many financial rods in the fire, really did help. I found myself with more energy and I also became much less scattered." I then asked: "And how did you find that Mercury change?" She then said: "Well, I think this was a tad harder than the other changes that I'd experienced. But, just knowing that I was supposed to become more boringly logical and learn to be more dry and intellectual, helped me to do this." I then said: "I understand. Just know that are planets are like muscles in our bodies. We can very profoundly improve these different muscle-groups by putting more consistent attention on them.

CHAPTER 9

ASTROLOGY FOR THE SELF-HELP PROFESSIONALS!

"The purpose of life is to grow."

~ Maharishi Mahesh Yogi

One of the greatest ways in which our entire culture can most profoundly benefit from both of these two most major consciousness and astrological breakthroughs – is if this greatest area of life today – these so-called Self-help professionals can find themselves benefiting the most from these two greatest of breakthroughs.

These self-help individuals, by the way are already some of the most important of all individuals in the world today, just because they are even now caring for, nurturing, healing, guiding and instructing most of the rest of our world's population!So, whether you are one such healer, teacher, nurse, therapist, guide or light-worker, even parents; this chapter then here is written for YOU!

So, what is it that all such self-help individuals have in common?

#1 – They all want to first of all, understand 'why' their patients, clients or students, are going through what they are experiencing.

#2 – Secondly, they all, also want to figure out how 'best' to guide, instruct, teach and even enlighten their very same students. Regardless as to their exact perspective, gifts, knowledge or wisdom, they all want to help their clients to first become more self-actualized and as a result of this, become that much more successful and happy in this life. Let's now discuss how much of this new astrology can most profoundly, 'help' these self-help individuals help their patients and clients.

Parents – The First – Self-Help – Individuals – We should first mention our parents because they are without a doubt, in many ways, the most important of such self-help persons.

Because what do our parents seek to do?

They are there to first Understand us and then help, guide and lead us to become the most successful and happy adult versions of ourselves, possible!

They first try to understand us, what we are like and especially what our main human strengths and weaknesses are. Though, they don't have us for very long and fairly quickly end up passing us off to our teachers, still, what they do end up doing will literally set the stage for most of the rest of our adult lives.

And, now, because of this much more accurate and profound astrology which is coming into the world today, all such parents can quickly understand their children that much more quickly and right away begin better guiding and nurturing and nourishing their children!

Especially for all those parents who've only known about the western system of astrology before, discovering now just how much more accurately your children's eastern charts will fit them will be such a great benefit and blessing for your natural child-rearing. Also, because most parents are already so very motivated to help their children to grow and become more successful in their future lives, discovering now how astrology is much more capable and competent in these two essential ways will then make one's parenting just that much more easy as well as profound! Also, parent's too should learn their own charts because the extent to which they know 'how' their own, personal charts fit them, that than will give them that much more clarity as to then be able to help their children.

The Self-Help – Teachers – Guides – Instructors – Mentors - For me, my very first mentors in my life were my teachers. And, I only wish now that they had also, been astrologers! Then, they could have more deeply understood me and been able to better guided me to discover more quickly, "who" I was and what my essential life purpose was supposed to have been all about!

Of course all such teachers and self-help instructors, should also know their own personal charts because from that greater self-understanding and even 'wisdom' they will be able to much more profoundly guide and lead all of their students.

The Self-Help – Healers – Doctors – Physicians – Nurses – etc. – Even all such healing self-help professionals should know more about this new astrology which is coming into the world today. There is also such a huge, most profound healing advantages within this astrology because the real reasons why everyone creates both the health and ill-health that we are found living, can also be found right there within these same kinds of unique astrological reasons!

Most such self-help healers can know and teach all of their clients and patients about Saturn. Saturn is after all the #1 health planet and will be for most people, the most vital of all such healing tools and practices, just because the 'best' ways in which each one of us, is meant to 'heal' will be found within those unique details of our personal charts. There are also, 5 other Health components to be found within the unique details of each person's charts.

The Self-Help – Life Coaches – Mentors – Guides – Instructors

For all those who already think of themselves as such teachers and life-coaches, this new astrology will be particularly significant in terms of helping you better guide and lead your clients. Let's say, you are one such, vital Life-coach. And, you already are involved in helping people to discover 'what' they came into this life to achieve and to accomplish.

There is no such better or more profound 'life' tool than this astrology. And, though you do not have to become such a professional astrologer, still you can become one of the greatest of all such life-coaches simply by adding this wonderful astrological knowledge and wisdom to whatever other unique perspectives are such an intimate part of your present practice.

The exact life-purpose that we all came into this life to find and then to excel in can be found the most clearly and effortlessly within your client's charts!

Financial – Self-Help – Professionals – Those of you who have already such a vivid interest in helping your clients to achieve such important, greater financial success, will benefit the most profoundly with just such a greater appreciation of this same, astrology. Even those two unique 11th and 12th – financial Houses can give such a deeper insight into 'why' each of your clients are even now creating the unique, financial difficulties and challenges they have been experiencing!

And now that more of this all-important self-development potential of astrology is being revived today, all such financial advisers will be much better prepared to help all of their clients to achieve real financial freedom and abundance in this life!

The Self-Help – Psychologists – Psychiatrists – Therapists – Then there are those most important of self-help individuals who are the world's greatest of care-givers and include all such psychologists, therapists and even counselors. Because of all of these most changes and improvements going on within this entire field of astrology today, now for the very first time, we have a complete science of Human Psychology which will allow any and all such self-help, individuals to become the most successful of mental health professionals.

This will manifest for all such persons with this growing appreciation as to just how profoundly, "astrology is nature's psychology!" In other words, we can now see exactly why each person has the unique psychological personality that they each got born with. And also, why we each have the unique human problems and weaknesses that we are found living. And finally, because of this most important and profound astrological "self-development" breakthrough going on today, all such mental health professionals can also use this new astrology to help all of their patients and clients to dramatically self-improve and to grow, internally from this same astrology.

The Spiritual – Self-Help – Guides – Teachers & Gurus – Then there are those unique self-help individuals who have a uniquely "spiritual" orientation and perspective. This greatest of new astrology's that is coming into the world today, can have the most important and profound of spiritual influences for people too. My new, first Nature's Astrology books: "The Map of God – Astrology Is For Our Enlightenment" will give such self-help spiritual teachers the greatest, unique, spiritual knowledge and wisdom to allow all of their students to grow more profoundly within their spiritually than ever before.

There are even 5 essential "components" of spirituality that can be found in each person's individual astrological chart which will help all to #1) understand that unique Spiritual Nature that we each got born with and #2) How we're each meant to better understand the unique Spiritual Challenges that we each find ourselves experiencing in this life. And, 3) How one can even more easily see that unique Spiritual Path that each person is meant to be living and then finally, #4) We can most importantly find those unique Spiritual Solutions which will first of allow anyone to literally solve those unique Spiritual

Challenges that one had been experiencing and through this, finding that much more enlightenment and even God in this life, by practicing these unique astrological solutions!

All Other – So-Called – New Age – Self-Help Individuals – And finally, for all those who are also seeking to self-help and yet I have not been able to quite include your category here in this chapter, that unique and all-important self-help work that YOU have been doing, I'd like to include some final remarks.

All such self-help individuals will benefit tremendously by coming to understand this essential knowledge and wisdom of this new astrology because the unique Human Condition that each one of us is found living, can be the most clearly understood by shining this light of astrology upon each person's individual life. And one of the greatest of all such astrological insights is that there is a very real and undeniable "astrological link" between our very human lives and our personal astrological charts. In other words, for every human situation, whether one is looking at human strengths or weaknesses; but there is a very real and distinct, unique astrological configuration that so very profoundly fits those very same, human tendencies.

All who struggle due to an important lack of interior self-confidence, for example have this unique human problem because of having been born with one such, so-called negative Sun-planet as found within one person's unique astrological chart. Those that get born with equally as important mental and emotional problems w ill be found to have these unique human weaknesses because they too, got born with one such, so-called negative Moon-planet within their personal charts.

And even though you may not be a professional astrologer and you will have many other, unique ways in which your practice helps all such individuals; if you add this unique perspective of astrology to your practice, you will find an even greater ability to help, guide and heal your many patients and clients!

CHAPTER 10

HOW WE REALLY FULFILL OUR DESIRES!

"How we fulfill our desires depends on having a desire and then having enough (Saturn) silence to then allow that desire to get fulfilled."

~ Maharishi Mahesh Yogi

One of the most fascinating benefits that will be coming to us now, due to both of these two major breakthroughs will be in terms of literally 'how' we can better understand how such Human Desire works! For example, most in common culture today only know about that most basic and immature, Mars fighting for what we want, part of ourselves.

In truth there are such – 9-components of desires and all together have to be balanced and positive enough for such natural fulfillment of desire to happen! I'll never forget when I first learned that I had each of these 9-planets within myself and they basically constituted exactly 'how' I sought to fulfill my very desires, each and every day.

The Sun for example, is an extremely important part of how well we're able to fulfill our desires. Those that get born with just such more Sun, self-confidence will be much more capable of fulfilling their natural desires than say those who do not get born with as much, Sun, self-confidence!

Then there are those who get born with very real and demonstrable emotional and mental problems in their lives.

They have these because they also got born with one such, more negative or malefic Moon-planet within their human-natures. And, everyone knows already even, just how much our "emotions" influence our attempts to fulfill our desires. Those who are emotionally more distraught, who have many more Moon-anxieties, worrying and especially depression will find that all of these most basic Moon-problems, will most intensely undermine and sabotage one's natural attempts to fulfill one's very desires.

Even modern day psychology today understands well, this process of "sabotaging". Even psychology has found undeniable links between those very negative things that happen to us and are present and future lives which are a natural reflection of our past. Those that get neglected or abused when they are young, can't help but taking these very stressful scars into their future.

Even such important modern day scenarios like Post traumatic stress disorders, or PTSDs as they are called, are bringing to our attention just how significant and negative, such stressful experiences can be for our future lives.

What has been missing so far however, is how there is this all-important astrological component regarding what happens to us. Those that get neglected or abused by their fathers for example are those who will get born with one such more negative Sun-planet from within their personal astrology. While those on the other hand who have tensions and negative experiences related to their mothers, will be those kinds of individuals who got born with one such, more negative or malefic, Moon-planet from their personal astrology.

Not only do our personal planets from birth represent 'who' we are and 'why' we are the unique personality that we've long been living. But, these very same positive and negative planets within each person, can also describe most clearly that rather complete "desire" nature that each person, also got born with!

I remember when I first learned about this astrology and discovered my complete chart and where my most important positive and negative, birth planets were. This helped me immensely because at some point it also occurred to me, when I was young, I only really knew about the singular, Mars, aspect of desire.

What this means is that I just knew about how to Mars-take whatever I wanted! Being the oldest of six children in my family I just thought too that I Sun, deserved to get whatever I wanted. My mother however, being more adult and more grown up than I was; sensed what I needed. You would constantly say: "You know Mark you have to learn to share!"

I'd just tried Mars-taking something from one of my siblings and my mother came down on me with this very strange and mysterious statement. "I have to share?" What a peculiar idea this was to me. I knew that if I wanted something I just needed to Mars-take it. Though, none of us knew anything about astrology, at this time. My mother however, just knew that this is what I needed.

Unfortunately, I wouldn't ever quite get this for decades!

As it turns out my own, personal Venus, "sharing" nature was much less well-developed and it would be years before I'd realize that this was why, it didn't come so naturally to be, to understand that one needed to share! However, the very moment that I began to learn these things and especially which of my personal planets were strong and positive and which ones were more weak and negative; I began to 'see' so much more clearly, exactly where I needed to grow and self-improve within myself.

And from that very moment when I was able to grow and develop within say, my other Venus nature, it became that much more easily for me to 'share' and as a result, I was able to more easily fulfill my desires just because such a Venus-planet is also very much a part of our real, complete desire nature! In this chapter we are going to go into much more depth as to this slightly more elaborate and previously confusing, 9-components of desire and how our interior, planetary self-improvement is exactly what we all need to discover 'how' we can powerfully improve and strengthen our very desire natures in this life!

The Sun - #1 Component - We've already mentioned briefly how everyone gets born with one such, all-important Sun, self-confidence aspect to one's natural ability to fulfill our desires. This Sun part of us also represents how much self-worth and even, literal strength of will, we will each get born with! So, if you already recognize that you have been living with a dramatic lack of self-confidence or lack of self-worth, then by all means, know that your interior Sun-growth may just be one of the most important things you need to improve, in this life.

The Moon's - #2 – Component – Then there is this equally as important emotional Moon-component as to how we seek to fulfill our desires which represents how emotionally stable and steady we will be mentally, in our lives. We already know that people who are majorly neurotic, psychotic or mentally ill have a huge impediment in terms of their natural ability to fulfill their very desires!

So obviously, those who are 'insane' have the greatest difficulty because they are living under much delusion, maybe even hallucinations and certainly all kinds of emotional and mental problems. Even one's Moon-intuition is a part of how one seeks to fulfill one's desires. Though what has not been known until now however, is astrologically 'why'! But, now that we're able to much more profoundly see how these 9-components or planets of astrology really do define, exactly who we are; we can now see so much more clearly that these also, do represent how we each seek to fulfill our very desires.

The very moment, for example, when I began to better

212

understand that I'd also been born with one such more negative, Moon-planet within myself; I then began to realize just how much this human-weakness also really diminished my natural ability to fulfill my very desires! Later, however when I then began to meditate and discovered one such important way in which I might be able to strengthen and improve this very same, Moon-part of myself; I began to notice that right away, I could more easily and more profoundly fulfill my desires, than ever before!

And the more I understood my Moon and how it was one of my chief, most important of negative or malefic planets, I began to see just how much this natural human weakness part of me, did in fact, strongly undermine and sabotage myself and my natural desires and goals and wishes, in my life.

The Mercury - #3 – Component – Then there is that other equally as important other 'mental' side of our human natures, which we know of as our human intellects or left-brain parts of ourselves. Astrology on the other hand, has long called this part of us, our very personal Mercury natures! And how well we think, how crisp and clear is our intellectual reasoning and even how well we will be deciding, choosing and discriminating, are all natural reflections as the quality and positivity of our Mercury-intellects!

So, if you have already find that you have much intellectual confusion and a lack of clear, understanding; then look into this very important Mercury-part of yourself and see if you need to also grow and self-improve within this natural Mercury-part of yourself.

The Venus - #4 Component – Then there is that other important human planet which is called Venus. Our Venus planets represent how well-loved we will be growing up and how appreciative, giving and loving we will be in our lives. And, we all know instinctively that those who are better givers, who know how to share, appreciate and love; seem to be much more

213

happy and capable than those who get born with a very clear, lack of Venus-lovingness within their human-natures. I too got born with that much more disappointing and less well-developed Venus planet within my chart. But, the very moment when I learned this about myself and discovered how to become that much more whole and positive within this very same Venus part of me; this had the most surprising of effects, that I was able to get my desires fulfilled, much more easily!

The Mars – 5th – Component – We also briefly mentioned how Mars too is another important aspect to how we seek to fulfill our desires. Our Mars' is that exact part of us that will give us the physical energy and determination to fulfill our desires. This same Mars part of us will also give us a natural ability to stand up for ourselves which sometimes is also such an important aspect to our fulfillment of desire.

Those who don't know how to stand up for themselves and are instead taken advantage of or abused, most definitely find their natural desires being thwarted or diminished. And what is also so very important to know about one's inherent, interior Mars-nature is that Mars can be more negative or dysfunctional being either too hot or fiery or not fiery enough.

In other words, Mars' more negative side can come from an overly too intense and aggressive malefic nature. Or Mars' chief negativity can also come from a too Mars passive or timid kind of Mars, human nature. Also, the exact Sign and House placement that we find our Mars' planets 'in' will then define whether our personal Mars is negative or positive. When Mars is found within its 3 best of Signs, #1 Aries, #8 Scorpio or #10, exalted Capricorn; all three of these most positive of Mars placements will tend to represent one such, much more positive Mars part of oneself.

Those on the other hand, who get born under different, Mars-configurations will quite often find that their Mars is much more negative. And as a result of this, more negative Mars planet such individuals will also discover just how much this negative Mars-part of them, most intensely interferes with their natural desire to fulfill their very human desires.

WE see this all the time in the world today. Millions of people find themselves Mars-fighting, in disagreements, quarreling, angry and mad and all of this excessive Mars-vibrations most definitely is not helping either of these parties to fulfill their very desires, more easily!

One's Jupiter – 6th – Component – Then there is this other, just as important Jupiter part of us which on the surface, represents how much good luck or divine grace we will each get born with. And we all sense that there just might be this very strange and kind of mysterious 'luck' feature which is even now, so intimately involved with our fulfillment of desire.

Also this very same, Jupiter part of us represents how open and accessible we will be to "knowledge and wisdom" in our lives. And those who do have greater access to important wisdom and knowledge will find that they are able to much more easily fulfill their desires. Those on the other hand, who find themselves more closed down to knowledge, who live a kind of more 'ignorant' human-situation, most definitely find themselves experiencing all kinds of almost innumerable problems and difficulties in terms of how they seek to fulfill their natural desires.

The Saturn - #7 – Component – Then there is this equally as important, other so-called spiritual planet which is called Saturn which then represents that interior part of us that is either balanced or imbalanced. Those who wake up refreshed and Saturn-raring to go will find that their days go much more easily and their able to much more naturally fulfill their very desires.

Those on the other hand, who find themselves with all kinds of stressed situations, imbalances, tension, fatigue and dis-ease will then find out just how much these Saturn-imbalanced situations really do undermine and sabotage one's desires in addition to undermining and sabotaging one's very health!

The Rahu-Ketu - #8 – Component – Then there is a final Rahu and Ketu aspect to our desires. Though, Rahu and Ketu are not real planets out there, they do refer to very real astronomical realities which we know of as these eclipses of each year. Rahu & Ketu then, represent how close our own, personal date of birth was to one of these two major eclipses that happen each year.

Also, such eclipses are known to be a reflection as to just how pure and positive our very "desires" are, in this life. Those that get born with a much more negative Rahu-Ketu nature will then find themselves with all kinds of distorted desires like, addictions, compulsions and obsessive tensions and bad habits in their lives. Therefore, such individuals who do find themselves with such "addictions" will then most definitely discover how these, so totally interfere with one's natural desire, to fulfill one's natural desires!

Conclusion – The more we each discover now, that what is really going on within ourselves, is that we are always, living these very same, 9-planets within our very human natures; we'll then be able to much more clearly understand why we are also experiencing the lack of fulfillment of desire which we've long been experiencing within our lives.

However, the very moment when we then discover how we can most significantly and powerfully self-improve and even, self-develop these very same planets; then we will have begun experiencing how we can also, most favorably, now begin improving our very real and auspicious, ability to naturally fulfill our desires. Regardless as to what human or earthly situation that we get born in. That very moment when we're able to improve our very real, interior planets; from that very moment we'll find such a greater, ability to fulfill our desires!

CHAPTER 11

LEARNING YOUR OWN, PERSONAL CHART!

"You will be your own best Jyotishee (astrologer)."

~ Maharishi Mahesh Yogi

One of the most powerful and significant 'ways' that we can each take such greater advantage of both of these two most powerful and significant of breakthroughs – is for you to personally, learn all about your own, astrological chart.c

This is particularly significant because in the past, very few, individuals ever knew anything about their charts. In fact, most of this astrology that was practiced was that which was done by these so-called professional astrologers and their students. Very rarely however, were these students then, 'taught' more about their personal charts.

Two Kinds Of People In the World!

I've found that there are basically two kinds of people in the world. There are those who don't really understand that much about their personal charts. And, then there are those who've made a point of discovering for themselves, how their own, personal charts do in fact, profoundly fit them!

There is such a profound difference in such individuals and those who come to understand more deeply, 'how' their charts already fit them will find that they automatically receive more advantages and more benefits than those who don't understand their personal charts. It is therefore such a fortunate situation in the world today, because within this fine art and science of astrology today, it is now known to be that much more easy and effortless to learn one's own, personal astrology. I see too that there have been two, seemingly unrelated, other modern day technological breakthroughs which have also contributed to this greater tendency for people to be able learn their own charts, now.

2 Modern Day Technological Breakthroughs!

#1 – The Computer - For example, with this creation of computer, this has also seriously influenced astrology. Now, millions have been able to learn their own charts, just because individuals created astrological software so that people could now calculate their own charts. This then made such astrological "self-learning" much more easy and effortless than ever before!

#2 – The Internet - Also with the creation of the Internet, we've begun to see such an expansion of huge numbers of individuals being able to study and learn their own charts, much more easily. The Internet too, also allowed hundreds of millions of individuals to become aware of the great depths and profundities of astrology, within their own traditions.

Also, millions have begun to become aware of the astrology of "the other", as well. This means millions in the west, have now become much more significantly aware of that essential astrology from the east. And, just as many, millions of individuals from the east, have now began to become much more aware of that unique western system of astrology and its many gifts and benefits.

And, finally due to this mutual "looking", both of these two very different astrological traditions have now begun rubbing off on each other and as a result of this more "mutual" appreciation, a very real, greater unification has begun within both of these systems.

This is the most profound because for hundreds and thousands of years, very little of the many diverse and different systems of astrology were much integrated into one 'wholeness' of astrology.

And, because the universe itself is only one universe and there is only one astronomy and there is only one "set of laws" of nature; there is really only one, unified, seamless, reality of astrology "out there."

But, the fact, that we've still had 2, 3 and even 4 very different and unintegrated systems of astrology in the world, being very active; this entire oneness of astrology has not been very appreciated.

Today, very fortunately; literally all of these very diverse and slightly different, systems of astrology are beginning to be understood in terms of becoming now, 'one' wholeness of astrology.

In the western system which had stood relatively unchanged for over 1600 years, now suddenly in the span of one generation, this very ancient system has begun, profoundly changing! Sixty years ago now, one lone western astrologer by the name of Cyril Fagan first suggested that we completely abandon that traditional western system of astrology and now adopt a completely, 23-degree different western system which he came to call Sidereal western astrology.

Today, so many millions of western astrologers and students and enthusiasts have begun learning about this new western system; that now, that previous, traditional western astrology is beginning to be understood as Tropical western astrology.

I'll never forget when I first became aware of this very new and quite different Sidereal western astrology. By now, I'd not only learned traditional western astrology but also eastern astrology and how much more accurately my eastern chart really fit me.

My first reaction was: "Oh, no, now there are 4 major systems of astrology existing in the world. Now, there are two western systems and one, traditional eastern or Jyotish system and many all over the world still study and quite revere the ancient eastern, Chinese system of astrology. And, if you throw in that most ancient Mayan system of astrology which became quite famous and quite the rage in 2012 when that so-called "astrological convergence" was supposed to be happening; we now have 5 major systems of astrology all vying for our attention!

Then it occurred to me: "You know with this introduction of this very new and fundamentally different Sidereal western astrology, because this system is much more accurate with that traditional western astrology; this then means that "astrology" is now beginning to be more integrated.

And, finally, much within that traditional eastern system has also begun very fundamentally changing. The second chief different between these two, historical western and eastern systems has been that quite a bit greater "fatalism" existed in the eastern system. As a result of this, this was quite different than the west, which had a much more positive and up-beat perspective.

Therefore, as both of these traditional systems began to better understand and appreciate each other, that very important and significant co-mingling began to then literally rub off on each other.

Many in the west began to take much of the eastern system that was more accurate and profound. Not only does one's eastern chart fit one much more profoundly but also, such very different eastern systems like the ancient Dasha system, haven't existed at all within the traditional western system.

And, where so much of the ancient eastern system had been so very fatalistic in the past; now, much more of that positive, up-beat and optimistic perspectives of western astrology have begun to rub off on that very same, traditional eastern system. You can see this so very clearly in the natural advertisements of many such eastern astrological websites on the net. Whereas even 25 years ago, most such eastern astrology books that were written were 'full' of this very distinct and quite stifling 'fatalism' which translated as the very real idea that one's chart is kind of "written in stone" and is incapable of being either changed and improved.

Now, on many such modern day eastern web sites, you'll hear such completely new and exciting ideas as: "Learn how to improve your family life. Discover how to make more money. And even, improve your health and even find God in this life!

And the greatest of changes going on today is how for the very first time, both of these two ancient systems of astrology are beginning to realize that we can now use our astrology to most profoundly, self-improve and self-develop ourselves!

See, in the past, more of the "diagnostic" nature of astrology, predominated. In both of these two, most widely practiced western and eastern systems; each of these have endeavored to explain to millions of people, how their personal charts, do in fact, most profoundly fit them! Very little has been written about as to 'how' one is also supposed to be able to improve oneself by learning how to improve one's very real, personal planets.

Though, there is some sense in the western system that such self-improvement might be possible. You'll hear this echoed in some western astrology books in such examples where the astrologer is talking to one of his students. In this one example, the student was complaining about the fact that he had a very intense accident prone nature that was making him have many, very horrible accidents.

The western astrology then said: "This accident prone nature that you've been experiencing is due to a very negative, Mars planet within your personal astrology. And, if you can discover how to improve this very same Mars-part of yourself then you might be able to improve this same, accident prone nature that you've been suffering with.

Within the traditional eastern system however, very little of this possibility is hardly ever considered. Whereas most such traditional eastern books only included that very diminishing "written in stone" quality and the inevitability of fate, because one can't really change or improve one's planets; only very rarely is even such planetary self-improvement considered.

For example, in all of the many, almost fifty eastern astrology books that I had, at some point; only one of these even mentioned this idea of planetary remedies and remedial measures. And, this one book of 200 pages, all about 'how' one's uniquely eastern chart, will profoundly fit one, only had 5 insignificant pages at the end of the book on such planetary techniques of planetary self-improvement!

Even I with my least astrological understanding at the time, thought that there was something wrong with this. Five out of 200 pages means only about 2.5% of the book was about how one might in fact, profoundly improve one's planets. Even I thought: "You know it would be much more effective to have at least 50% of such books be about 'how' we can most importantly and powerfully self-improve ourselves.

Alas, due to that very intense fatalism even much of these ideas as to how one might be able to improve one's planets, has been greatly missing and predominantly not even available in most of traditional astrology.

However, now as both of these systems continue to co-mingle and rub off on each other and become more and more integrated together, more and more of this all-important self-development nature and potential of astrology is beginning to be explored and quite wonderfully, taken great advantage of!

My own astrology is almost 80% self-development oriented!

Now, whenever anyone asks me a question and wants to know if there are any ways that they can improve their lives; I'll spend 20% of the time, explaining 'how' this person's chart, profoundly fits them. Then, I'll spend most of the time even up to 80% of the time, then discussing how they can most powerfully, self-improve and self-develop their own, personal planets.

Conclusion – With such a greater emphasis on millions of people learning their own charts, this greater tendency today is allowing hundreds of millions of people now, to much more deeply appreciate exactly how their personal charts, really do fit them. And as these and many more equally as important and profound, changes and improvements within astrology continue to become more and more available; this over-all state of astrology in the world today, is rapidly becoming even that much more favorable and auspicious.

The last thing I'd like to say about this 'new' astrology that is happening today, is 'why' this greater self-learning is so very important. My own favorite guru echoed this idea one time when he said: "You all will be your own best Jyotishee." And, though I also knew he also meant 'be your own best astrologer'; later I realized why it is so very vital that we all, learn how our own charts profoundly fit us!

Astrology is truly what is considered to be one such, most profound "subjective" science. This means it's meant to be learned in and by oneself. In the same way that meditating and becoming more consciousness-enlightened is also meant to be so self-learned. Astrology is meant to be so, self-learned and becomes infinitely more effective and profound than those who merely 'hear' about their personal astrology!

This is very great, good news of course because one of astrology's greatest of problems has been that there are way too many different and unintegrated, systems of astrology from all over the world. And, because the universe itself, only lives one astronomy and one set of laws of nature; there can really be only one, natural reality of astrology which exists in life.

There then, having been so many different and in many ways, opposed systems of astrology before; this has only contributed to the lack of astrological sophistication and lack of efficiency and the lack of capabilities that too many systems of astrology found themselves experiencing.

Now, that hundreds and hundreds of millions of people are becoming that much more knowledgeable and sophisticated in terms of this very astrology; this greatest of astrological research projects is already having the most profound effect on astrology itself first. And, very quickly, our entire world and human-culture will also be so very dramatically and powerfully improved just because…..

As it turns out… we have always been such "Astrological Beings ….living in this very real, and significant Astrological Universe…in which we live!

And this entire process today of millions of such individuals learning their own charts, is greatly improving this entire field of astrology as a result.

There is too one final other reason why such greater self-learning is now having such a profound influence on individuals and astrology alike. As one of my favorite gurus used to say:

"You all will be your own best Jyotishee" (astrologer)

His Holiness Maharishi Mahesh Yogi

And though I didn't quite understand this expression before. A number of years later after I'd been researching and exploring this Maharishi concept of astrology and enlightenment for many years, one day I then had this most amazing experience of becoming my own best astrologer!

I ran into a friend of mine who knew much more about astrology than I did. And, when I told him about my most recent trip to India and studying astrology with the Maharishi he then offered to look at my chart. He then went into many aspects of my chart, how it fit me, how it fit my personality and even my major, strengths and weaknesses.

This time, however, I could follow his reasoning since I'd now been studying those same astrological rules in which he had previously studied. Then, he finished by concluding with some final remarks, which quite surprised me! Though, he'd been completely right-on before in terms of how he analyzed my chart, still in his final words, I realized there was something 'off' about his thoughts. Then, it occurred to me: "Oh, my God, I have become my own, best astrologer." This means of course, not that we will always be the most technologically knowledgeable about our charts. This just means we're supposed to be more self-referral and learn our own charts. And, when we do, we'll rise up to such a higher appreciation than ever before.

Conclusion – Therefore, as soon as you can, one of my most eager suggestions for everyone is to come to study and learn about your own charts. Especially, since you were born with that unique astrological human, nature that you've long been living; you are already in the best position to know your own chart, just because you've always, already been living it!

And, when you hear about that or read about it, you will then have such a deeper experience of your own chart, most profoundly fitting you, just because you are already living that!

CHAPTER 12

ASTROLOGY IS NATURE'S PSYCHOLOGY!

"The puzzling thing is that there is really a curious coincidence between astrological and psychological facts."

~ Carl Jung

Then one day I had this most surprising and exquisite realization:

"Oh, my God, astrology is nature's natural, psychology!"

By now I'd already learned how my unique eastern chart really did fit me, as well as how all of my family members and friend's charts fit them too. I'd even studied how about 200 to 300 other people's charts also fit them as well and then one day realized: "I now know how one's chart is such a clear description of that unique human personality and natural, psychological tendencies that one got born with!

And if you also include the fact that one's own chart will also be able to describe so very clearly why one also is found living those essential human strengths and weaknesses, that one gets born with, then you can realize: "This is all pure psychology!"

The first thing that one can say about this most important and unique application of astrology, is that our very real human personalities and human strengths and weaknesses are all, right there within these unique details and planetary configurations of our personal charts. Why one person gets born with so many important emotional and mental problems can now be found very clearly in those very same, so-called, negative Moon-configurations of their charts. Other individuals who get born with quite a bit of lack of personal self-confidence, has this very important human problem doe to being born with one such negative Sun planetary configuration within their charts.

Those too who find themselves experiencing important 'health' problems, even of a physical kind will find that there is such a unique Saturn reason as to 'why'. And, for those who find themselves experiencing all kinds of typical, psychological anxieties, fears, paranoia and especially depression; almost always, all of these will be found deeply imbedded in those so-called more negative Moon-configurations within our charts.

One of my brothers and I both got born with such negative Moon-configurations within our individual charts. And the fact that my small Moon, one that was very negatively positioned due to being in my 12th House and being so very close to my Saturn planets; did profoundly help me to see why I'd been born so very shy, self-conscious and with so many human worries, anxieties and depression. And perhaps if I'd also been born into a more wealthy family, my parents might have sent me to professional psychologists to try and help me.

My brother too got born with his own, brand of Moon problems, though none of us quite saw this until years later. When he went to college he had a nervous breakdown and got branded as being schizophrenic! He never did figure out how to significantly or profoundly self-improve his very important Moon nature. Where I was much more lucky. Though, I probably had just as potentially dangerous and negative psychological, Moon-condition within my chart, I had one positive than my brother did not.

My slightly better Jupiter-planet allowed me to attract to myself such all-important self-development technologies as meditating, yoga and Ayurveda and especially meditating right away began improving this very same, Moon part of myself which then right away began so profoundly self-improving my very own, initial birth, psychological nature and condition.

In the very near future, we'll begin to realize that there have been two such most recent human, breakthroughs that are going to have the most immediate and profound of effects upon the entire field of astrology.

#1 – With this greater appreciation of the much more accurate and precise eastern astrology, we can now quite exactly, identify "why" every single human being gets born with the unique psychological nature and condition that they are living.

#2 – However, what's even more important than being able to discover 'why' each person is struggling and suffering with those unique emotional and mental problems that they have been experiencing; is how we can now do something profound and important to dramatically self-improve and self-develop ourselves!

#3 - And as we learn how to do this, that much more deeply important, higher potential of astrology to become a profound science of human potential; will then become the chief way in which psychology will be experienced, in the very near future.

With these 3 main benefits now, that so very vital science of human Psychology will suddenly become more fulfilled and complete!

Take any person's life but now examine what they are going through, in the light of their personal astrology and you can easily and quickly discover 'why' they have been struggling and suffering in the unique ways that they have. Whereas quite a bit of traditional astrology has spent so much time trying to analyze 'why' the person has the unique emotional difficulties that they have been long living.

Today, one can simply look at their charts and in 5-minutes

discover 'why'. After this one can then spend a couple of hours working with the person and in 'doing' their astrological readings with them, come to help them to also understand 'why'. Once one then discovers why one is struggling and suffering in the unique psychological ways that one has been living, of course it is even much more important that we also discover 'what' we can now do differently to significantly improve our very same, particular emotional and mental situation that we've long been living.

I had this same realization from the very first moment when I learned from my personal astrology chart, 'why' I had the very frustrating and debilitating emotional and mental difficulties that I'd long been suffering with. However, what was different for me was the fact that I then was able to find such important and profound ways in which I could learn 'how' to strengthen and develop, this very same, Moon-part of my inner psyche, which then quickly made me much more self-actualized then I would have ever thought possible.

It will also be good to know that there are two primary aspects of one's astrology which deals with one's very, human psychology. There is this Moon-planetary part of us which directly describes how emotionally stable or 'insane' we will be. Then, there is an equally as important Mercury-part of our inner lives which describes how well our intellectual, minds will be doing.

Some people struggle psychologically because of the unique Moon-planets and Moon-configurations that existed within their astrology charts, from birth. Other such individuals will find themselves struggling and suffering because of that uniquely as negative so-called Mercury-negative configurations that they were born with.

You can also think of both of these planets as representing what modern day science today calls the Left & Right brains. That Left-brain part of us which is very representative of our linear thinking, rational mind and intellectual part of ourselves; astrology simply calls this our Mercury-planet!

And that equally as important Right-brain part of our inner lives; traditional astrology has long called the Moon-part of our inner psyches. This Moon-emotional part describes how stable and even and even mature we will be mentally and whether or not we'll have any such emotional challenges as excessive worrying, anxieties, fear, paranoia and even depression!

However, the greatest of all changes going on now, within especially astrology is 'how' we can now, most profoundly and relatively easily; significantly self-improve and self-develop these very two, most important psychological parts of ourselves. As a result of this, now modern psychology can not only quickly identify 'why' the person is struggling and suffering in those uniquely psychological ways.

But, now they can quickly discover 'how' they can most profoundly heal and improve these very psychos which have been such a natural focus of most psychological practices.

There is too that 3rd most profound benefit and advantage of using one's very astrology in such an important psychology way. This is how we can also, most significantly self-improve and self-develop literally, all of our personal planets which then have the most extraordinary effect of literally, unfolding more and more of one's latent potential.

And finally we should mention one final aspect of one's psychology which is represented by one's very important, consciousness nature. Every single human being gets born with an interior, very real and significant state of consciousness which they are therefore living.

As it turns out both this consciousness and our astrology, define the most clearly, that exact human psychological nature that each person is born with. So, in addition to discovering 'how' one can improve one's very mind by learning how to strengthen one's mental-planets, we also should spend as much time as possible expanding and improving our very consciousnesses which is that final aspect of one's very psyche.

We're also so very fortunate today, because there have been just as mind, most recent breakthroughs in this traditional field of consciousness as there have been in that equally as important astrology field. Take that most recent, consciousness breakthrough which is simply called Transcendental Meditation. This is particularly profound because this very new, technique today is bringing such profound and extraordinary changes and improvements within the field of consciousness, because now, for the very first time; now millions of people are very quickly and most profoundly unfolding the full potential of consciousness within themselves, which previously took decades and decades of constant attention.

What is the most unique about this very special T.M. technique then is that this is the first consciousness-expansion technique which recognizes that such awareness expansion can be completely easy and effortless! This effortless by the way, is the central benefit and profundity of this very unique expansion of consciousness technology.

Today, more individuals, millions of people have now learned how to most significantly expand their very consciousness than 'ever' before and this huge consciousness breakthrough is already beginning to have quite a huge impact on many people's psychological practices and concerns.

To be able to then have one's patients and clients learn how to meditate and significantly start unfolding one's innate consciousness will then go along way in immediately help the person dramatically self-improve their very same, mental condition. I, for one, was one such great example as to how my many, emotional and mental, Moon-difficulties could immediately be lessened and improved, from simply then meditating. And, later when I learned how to add, this equally as important and profound 'astrological' component to my mental growth; that then had an even more profound of influences. Because what astrology can uniquely bring to one's very psychology is, #1 – 'why' one has been previously living those unique mental and emotional, psychological challenges that one has been living.

With such a deeper appreciation then as to 'why' and then that even greater ability to discover 'how' one can most profoundly self-improve; then this entire field of astrology will become infinitely more complete and profound! Because we are in fact, truly consciousness and astrological, psychological beings and when we finally realize this; we will come to understand what psychology is really all about.

Let's now look into a ladies chart her and see if we can find out exactly 'why' she got born with that unique psychological nature and situation she has long been living in her personal life!

She even came to me wanting to know 'why' she was having the unique human, mental difficulties she'd long been experiencing. She said this: "Mark, I've come to understand from following your newsletters that our astrology is supposed to be able to express any kinds of psychological issues that one will end up experiencing in our lives. Is this true? For example, I've long been feeling quite good on some level but at the same time, experiencing quite a deep and very frustrating lack of self-confidence in my life."

I of course love hearing people's exact words because you can literally 'hear' their personal charts 'speaking' when you learn how people's exact words ARE their personal charts, speaking. So, when she said she had been feeling relatively 'good' that then made me think that perhaps her Moon-planet might be better. While at the same time, when she mentioned a lack of "self-confidence" I immediately thought this might refer to a more difficult or negative Sun-planet and configuration going on within her personal chart. So, I thought it was very fascinating that literally both of these very conditions that she had mentioned could be found literally, in those unique Moon and Sun details of our her personal chart. Even such traditional astrology has long said that such a unique Sun-configuration as here, her Sun or "Su" in the 12th House and within that unique #Sign of Libra are two such Sun-conditions that will almost

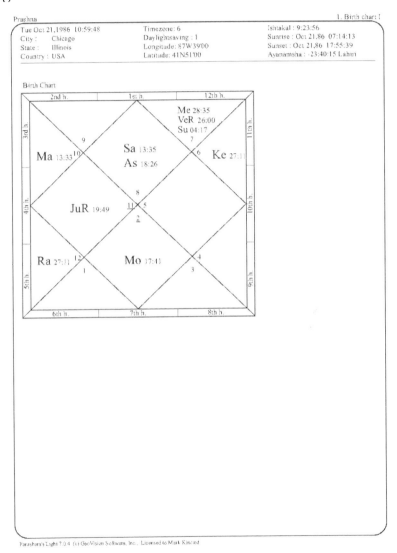

Prashna

Tue Oct 21,1986 10:59:48	Timezone: 6	Ishtakal : 9:23:56
City : Chicago	Daylightsaving : 1	Sunrise : Oct 21,86 07:14:13
State : Illinois	Longitude: 87W39'00	Sunset : Oct 21,86 17:55:39
Country : USA	Latitude: 41N51'00	Ayanamsha : -23:40:15 Lahiri

Birth Chart

Bring such a unique lack of self-confidence into one's life. And, that situation too when she said, she felt relatively 'good' I found this equally as fascinating because as you can see in her chart, here, too; she'd been born with that very good Moon-planet which is that "Mo" in the box with the #2 Sign of Taurus. The Moon or mental side of one is said to be the most positive and well-developed when the Moon is found in its most favorable and even, 'exalted' Sign of Taurus.

I did however, notice that she also had a more negative Saturn planet or that "Sa" in her chart, directly opposite to her so-called better Moon-planet. This then made me think that she might also have some degree of depression, sometimes though this was due, uniquely to Saturn's influence than the general state of her Moon-planet.

I was also curious to look into that second major aspect of one's mental situation which is one's Mercury planet. And, for this I then discovered that her, "Me" was also very poorly placed within that same 12th House and within that typically more negative #7 Sign of Libra. Many such Mercury in Libra individuals find that they have such unique intellectual issues and challenges because of their Mercury planet being deposited in this unique #7 Sign of Libra.

So, we began discussing all of these unique aspects of her chart, though what most such individuals really need to learn is 'why' they've been presently struggling and suffering in the unique ways that they have. I then told her that the Sun represents self-confidence while the Moon, how emotionally happy we will be. Also, we discussed Mercury's other, mental role in our lives.

We then went into much more detail as to just how she would be living that unique lack of Sun, self-confidence that she had even, initially described. For example, when I describe the Sun, more negatively positioned within this unique Sign of Libra, I said this: "Typically, the Sun ends up being less positive and indicative of more ego and I, self-confidence difficulties because the Sun doesn't really like being in this unique Sign. In other words, the very nature of Libra is so very different and in many ways, opposed to the very nature of the Sun; so such individuals will find themselves experiencing quite a bit of lack of Sun, self-confidence."

We then also went into much more detail as to how such a unique Sun-Libra pattern could be experienced by one and for this I then said: "The Sun in Libra is more negative than say other Signs because one's Sun nature becomes more negative when found in that constantly vacillating nature of Libra."

She then asked: "Can you explain this more?" I then said: "Libra's nature is to seek harmony and balance in life. And, one of the chief ways that it does this is by 'seeing both sides' of pretty much any and every issue, in life. Libran's experience this as a constant back and forth quality.

I for example, got born with a #7 Libra Rising Sign and from the very moment I read about Libra, I realized I did have this most unique Libra quality of being able to 'see' the other side. So, if a person was putting forth a uniquely liberal agenda, my Libra part of me would be found thinking of the pro's and con's of this and that complete opposite conservative point of view at the same time.

I found this kind of surprising because generally, I thought of myself as being a kind of more liberal type of person. But, somehow I also had this ability to 'sense' the other point of view. This then being one of the central, chief qualities of Libra, then can be experienced in such positive or negative ways. I found that I was living more of the more positive side of Libra. Though, over the years I found many of Libra clients and students were living much more of the negative side of Libra.

One such Libra person who also had his Sun and Mercury planets within this same Sign of Libra, reported to me, that this vacillating quality was so strong in him, he couldn't even make up his mind in terms of picking his toothpaste. He's spent hours looking at all the possible toothpastes that were available and going back and forth as to these various pro's and con's of each toothpaste! I said to him: "This is due to your many planets, more negatively positioned within this unique #7 Sign of Libra. The solution then for you, will be to discover 'how' you can improve this part of yourself and your very Sun-Libra nature.

And as you do this then such an important improved, human, self-confidence will be your reward!"

This lady and I then talked about that other chief, quality that her personal Sun was involved in which was that unique 12th House that it was found deposited in. I first explained the essential nature of this 12th House and quite often it is even described as the main House of Loss, in one's life.

In fact, individuals who get born with such unique planets here will be born at 'loss' with these very same planets. I even described how I had this very same situation in my chart and both my Moon and Saturn planets that were there within my 12th House, described to me that I too had been born at 'loss' to these two Moon and Saturn parts of my inner life.

She then said: "I can totally relate to what you are saying. Now, that you mention this I see that there has been such a quality of loss around my very sense of self and now I begin to see that maybe this is why I have such a real, experience of such a lack of self-confidence."

I then said: "Once you discover for yourself just how your own, personal planetary configurations are so very indicative of what you're in fact, going through in this life; then you can to not only better understand yourself but then you'll begin to realize, 'what' now needs to be done differently and 'how' one is supposed to significantly self-improve and self-develop within ones very self! We then of course spent quite a bit of time as to just how she could be improving this very same, Sun part of her inner life and how there were both holistic and general techniques for the Sun's improvement as well as other, specific ways which were directly related to these very same details of her own chart. In other words, these two unique flavors of her chart, her Sun being in Libra and also in her 12th House, then were two such examples of 'specific' techniques for Sun-improvement that were unique to her chart and her chart alone.

We than had an equally as important discussion as to just how her Mercury planet could be also improved and strengthened.

I didn't hear from her for a few months but then when she did get back in touch with me, she had this to say: "Mark, I just wanted to tell you how much I enjoyed our readings together. They were particularly illuminating!

And, as I tried to practice those simple Sun techniques you mentioned, I began to feel such a strange and yet so very wonderful Sun-change within me! I suddenly felt like I was no longer, so intensely undermining my self-confidence and instead began to feel so very powerful within my very, Sun-self-nature!"

I then said: "That's great. And any other changes?" She then said: "Well, I noticed how much my Mercury intellect also improved and that other Moon-planet we talked about; helped me to see, where I had a previously, more well-developed part of me which I then could access and even take greater advantage of."

I've of course had other just as satisfying and fascinating, "mental health" situations improving for people. Take this next chart directly below for example. This chart was the chart of a man who came to me with just such important emotional and mental difficulties that he'd long been experiencing. He even said: "I've always felt quite uneven and with quite a bit of very real and striking emotional and mental difficulties. I find that I worry quite a bit and I also experience quite a bit of anxieties as well as quite a bit of depression too. So, when I heard from one of your lectures, how we can dramatically improve all such mental challenges experiences that we might find ourselves experiencing; I thought I should ask you to help me, if at all possible."

I then explained how astrology does in fact, have this great ability to first, 'diagnose' why we are each struggling and suffering in the unique ways that we do. I then mentioned that such a new, self-development breakthrough in astrology will now give us that equally as important, new ability to dramatically improve and strengthen one's most negative and less developed of personal planets.

We then began going into those unique details of his chart which I thought just might be the most relevant for him. As you can see in his chart, here next, that he too had been born with a much more negative or dysfunctional Moon-planet in his chart.

Since I already knew that this Moon or "Mo" in our personal charts is so very clearly indicative of how emotionally stable we will be; I found it particularly fascinating that this man had been born literally on a New Moon day!

That can be found as his "Mo" in the same box or Sign where his Sun or "Su" was. As you can see both his Sun and Moon are in that same #10 Sign of Capricorn in his chart and also notice how they are extremely too close too, only separate by 2 degrees. This huge Sun-combustion as it is called, then almost always means the kind of person who will get born with such Moon issues and difficulties and emotional and mental problems.

After we talked about this he then said: "Well, that's me! I do feel so very emotionally stunted and I find it equally interesting that my Moon-planet is also in that unique #10 Sign of Capricorn ambitiousness. I have always been soooo very ambitious oriented." I then said: "Even one planet in Capricorn can bring this intense quality of natural, ambitiousness.

And quite of bit of this can be natural and positive for one. But, the Moon here is much more negative just because its 'Size" is so small and indicative of such an important Moon-strengthening that one came into this life to find." He then said: "I can hardly wait!" I've always loved helping people the most with such negative Moon and Saturn planets. Because I, too got born with just as dysfunctional Moon and Saturn parts of

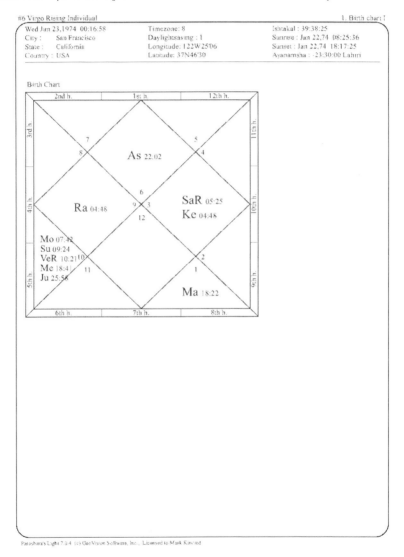

Inner life and yet I've also learned how to so significantly grow and self-improve in these very same ways; now I realize how helpful my experiences can be for others. We then began discussing how there were both holistic and specific ways in which one could most profoundly strengthen and self-improve one's very Moon nature and again he said: "Okay! I'm ready. Lay it on me!"

We began first starting talking about such holistic ways which include 1) meditating, which by the way is the #1 way in which one's interior Moon-mental part of oneself can be so very dramatically and powerfully improved. We also talked about how one can 2) put more important attention on one's interior Moon-needs. This Moon part of us represents how capable we will be to care, express compassion and even how motherly we will be; so one can then strengthen one's very Moon-self by choosing to care more and be more compassionate and motherly to oneself."

He then asked: "But, if this Moon-caring part of me is weaker, how can I do this, you know strengthen this very part that is itself so very weak?" I then said: "Number one, first strengthen the Moon by meditating and literally expanding the mind. Then, in addition, after meditating for a short while, make the point of consciously choosing to nurture, care and be more compassionate and motherly for oneself."

I knew that this might feel strange or slightly difficult for him so I also said: "Don't worry, just take it a step at a time. First learn how to meditate and right away this Moon part of you will dramatically improve." He then said: "Any other Moon gems you might suggest?" I then said: "Now that you mention this, there is one other extremely profound technique I found for literally expanding one's Moon mind. You've heard of the Moon's waxing and waning cycles before haven't you?"

He then said: "Eh, sure, I ... think so." I then said: "There are these two Moon cycles. Two weeks of each month, the inherent

240

light of the Sun will be found increasing and then culminating with the Full Moon. And two weeks the Sun's sunlight will be found decreasing in light. What I've learned about these two cycles is just how much more in-tune one can be with these very same, Moon-rhythms.

I even tell me: 'Make a point of watching these two Moon-cycles for two or three months in a row. Then, as you discover for yourself just how different these are; make a point of being more rest and recuperative oriented especially when the Moon is found waning and then do more and be more naturally active when the Moon is found waxing. And, this one simple exercise will do more for helping you to strengthen your Moon than ever before."

Conclusion – I then didn't hear from this man for about a year. But, after this time he got back in touch with me and had this to say: "Mark, I wanted to thank you for all you taught me. Especially when I learned how to meditate, right away I began to Moon-feel better. And as that change happened I was then able to even understand those other Moon suggestions you had mentioned and after a while began to practice these which then made my personal Moon feel more improved and more steady and stable than I would ever have thought possible!" I then said: "You now have such a profound Moon-mental formula for working on and improving your interior Moon-psychological part of yourself for the rest of your life!"

CHAPTER 13

FINDING THE LIFE YOU WERE BORN TO LIVE!

"If you travel the earth, you will find it largely divided into
two kinds of people – people who say, 'I wonder why such
and such is not done and people who say, 'Now, who is going
to prevent me from doing that thing!!"

- Winston Churchill

And as all of these many, so very exciting and profound new changes and improvements within astrology continue to become a part of our lives here on earth; one more just as exciting advantage will be this one:

"Oh, my God, this is the very reason why I was born!"

Everyone at some point in their lives wonders if there is such an inherently deep, life-purpose to which we are born. We however, rarely come to understand quite why we were born or if there was any kind of real, cosmic purpose to our lives.

When I was the youngest and growing up as a typical, innocent Christian boy I so very identified with the Christian idea that "the purpose of the Christian life was to strive to become an ever better and better person." Though, I had no idea how to do this, I did however find it quite meaningful to at least believe that this might be the very purpose of my life.

Later, when I then discovered how to meditate and began exploring that so-called "consciousness-expansion" reality, I then began to sense that my life purpose now was to become a very Christian, enlightened yogi! And this was quite fulfilling to sense that this hugely powerful, consciousness possibilities was deeply tied up with my very life-purpose.

However, the greatest clarity I ever received in terms of what my real-human purpose is all about; was when I then later, learned my own, personal chart.

In the beginning I first learned "How" my chart does it fact, profoundly fit me. Though, in 1977 when I only knew about that more fatalistic aspect of eastern astrology, I never got to that self-development possibilities. So, as a result, it never quite dawned on me that 'this' was why I'd been born.

And, though, at least now I at least knew 'why' I was that unique personality that I'd long been living, and yes, it was quite wonderful to at least know 'why' I also had those very same, human strengths and weaknesses that I'd been born with. However, I still didn't sense that this was really why I was born because I never could quite understand that one is most importantly 'born' because it is never enough just to live one's life, in the normal ways that we do.

We in fact, came here with a much deeper purpose. And, when we discover that this deepest of divine, cosmic purposes is to profoundly discover how to most fundamentally, self-improve and self-grow, well, that this is the most fulfilling.

As it turns out, the real purpose of our lives is our soul's, self-growth and when we finally realize this and begin experiencing this for ourselves, a time will come when we do begin to totally understand why we were born! Every single year from about 1989 where I began exploring and discovering more and more ways in which I could now be significantly self-improving and self, unfolding my very life; a time did finally come where I so very deeply realized: "Oh, my God this is why I was born!"

CHAPTER 14

THE PURPOSE OF LIFE IS OUR SOUL'S GROWTH!

"The purpose of life is to grow."

~ Maharishi Mahesh Yogi

And finally I'd like to end this most exciting Section by talking about how you can even discover how you can find that most amazing, deepest purpose of our lives which is to profoundly grow and self-transform within our very souls!

There are of course many goals, aspirations and purposes in life. In fact, each of those unique 12 Houses of one's astrology chart, literally define those very important, specific 'areas of the life' that one could be potentially interested in. There are Houses of family life, Houses of health and career and making money. In fact, all of the rather complicated and significant areas of the life will be found in all 12 of these very special Houses.

And exactly 'which' Houses we find our personal planets, will then define the most clearly exactly which areas of the life, are the most important and vital, for each one of us. So, in another sense we'll have to say that learning how to be more successful and happy in these unique areas will also be such an important part of one's very life-purpose!

However, what I've learned is that where we each got born with more positive and well-developed planets, we didn't really come into this life to grow or self-improve within these ways. In my own chart, those two, main positive planets that I had been born with; my Jupiter and Sun planets were my two chief, positives. And I did find that I didn't' need to so much change or improve within these planets. However, each of those other so-called more negative and malefic of planets, really do represent those very exact areas of our selves, that we came into this life to strengthen and self-develop!

And when we discover this, first exactly which planets are our least positive and most dysfunctional of negative planets but then learn how to most significantly and profoundly self-improve and self-develop, within ourselves; we will then begin to discover that this is really why I was born!

And even if you put more attention on improving such planets just because they had been more negatively influencing your career House or your Money Houses or even your romantic and relationship concerns. Still such self-growth is in fact at the very heart of why we came into this life. And as we make this all-important self-transformation; we will then discover the very deepest reason why we were born.

Because it is equally true to say, most of what happens here upon this earth, we can't take with us. We can't take our cars and fancy homes and business successes with us. In fact, all that we can take with us, is just how much soul-growth and how much self-growth we've been able to achieve!

We knew this before we came to this earth. And, we'll remember this again when we get to the other side. So, be sure you make such self-growth, a much higher priority in your life. And, you will be very happy that you did. Because not only will you be finally, much more in-touch with that very deepest, truest reason why we were born.

But, we will also become much more intimately capable and competent within those other, unique areas of the life that we're also so very interested in. Experiencing such career frustration not only draws our attention to those very important planets within our chart that are more negative. And as we learn how to strengthen and improve those very same planets that had been causing us such career-difficulties, we will then discover exactly 'how' we can most profoundly create such greater success within our careers.

But, this very same, planetary self-improvement will even more importantly end up fulfilling that very deepest human purpose which we came to find and explore, which is our very human self-growth and soul, self-transformation!

I used to feel really bad about my life because I was born with the most human weaknesses and dysfunctional aspects of my life. I long feel quite weak and majorly undeveloped and incapable in innumerable ways. However, every day that I realized that I could now be most profoundly self-improving and self-developing myself, I began to finally realize, this was a very great blessed life that I was born into, just because I had to self-improve and I had to self-develop!

In fact, when I was the youngest and found myself as a simple, Christian boy I first learned of this self-improving possibilities. I arrived home from church one day and I now had this most unusual Christian idea rambling around in my brain, that the true purpose of the Christian life is to become an ever better and better, more improved version of myself!

Though, there were no clear ways or means suggested at this time, I did however feel strangely changed and for the first time in my life thought: "I should make such human self-improvement a deeper part of my future life."

Later, when I then discovered western astrology, I then became aware of my very small and negative, hugely dysfunctional Moon part of me, too. And, though there were no ways suggested here as to 'how' I might improve this most negative Moon-part of myself; at least I know knew so much more clearly that I was supposed to now be growing in this very unique and distinctive Moon part of my inner life.

That then led to meditating and the other 44 years of such great and profound consciousness expansion that I have now been able to achieve. And, somewhere during that time, 28 years ago now, that side trip to India where I then heard about that eastern astrological idea that we could also be using our charts to profoundly improve our very spirituality; then catapulted me to the deepest appreciation of that inherent self-growth that I so very needed to experience in this life!

Now, 28 years later of this has convinced me more than ever before, just how our personal charts are in fact, the most profound and extraordinary treatises on that essential self-growth and most important soul-growth that we came into this life to find and to experience.

And when we get to the other side and we've been able to make such self-improvement a much higher priority and importance we'll then realize: "Oh, my God, I have been able to fulfill that real reason why I came to the earth, which was to find such wonderful self-growth and most profound, soul, self-development!

It is of course, an added benefit to also find that such self-improvement can also help one to become equally more successful in all of those other unique areas of our lives which are then located as those unique Houses in which are planets were deposited when we were born.

Conclusion – Our personal charts then are the most profound and wonderful maps as that exact self-growth and soul, self-improvement that we came into this life to find and to then self-transform. And when we do this, we will feel more self-fulfilled than we would have ever thought possible….

Just find and keep in mind those unique Positive vs. Negative planetary differences in your chart. Where each of your negatives were, these then represent exactly where you came in, to grow and most profoundly self-improve.

Section 3

THE FUTURE LOOKS VERY BRIGHT!

"Life is a field of all-possibilities.` "

~ His Holiness Maharishi Mahesh Yogi

There has never been a brighter time for humanity, than now. Not only can we "put a man on the Moon" and create the most wonderful computers, cars and smart-phones, but today, more is being understood about the even more important "subjective" side of life than ever before!

In this final Section of the book here, we will conclude with how both of these two most important fields of subjective knowledge and wisdom, consciousness and astrology 9are now becoming modern day, true sciences of life!

Because of that most unique breakthrough which is happening even now, in terms of consciousness; that very unique, Transcendental Meditation experience, alone is vastly changing this entire field of consciousness now. And as a result of even this one change, a complete and unprecedented science of consciousness now is coming into our world, today.

Also, each of these so very important and significant changes and improvements that are going on within this entire field of astrology today, will be very quickly, having the most surprising and effect, on this subjective side of our inner lives. Every single human being, born in the world has both a very unique and special consciousness nature deep within, located at the core of our beings. And, then on the more surface values of our lives, we have that unique astrological, human nature and human, individual personality that we are also living.

Having such breakthroughs going on now, within both of these two most important aspects of our human subjectivity will then end up being the greatest of all changes, now. Though, we have been a primarily very materialistic and object-referral, outer kind of human civilization, until now.

Today, such a huge subjectivity revolution is now going on. We have for example, more millions of people today, enjoying and quite exploring that relatively new self-help field which is so much more prevalent and important, today.

These two most important consciousness and astrological revelations will then do more for bringing such a deeper appreciation to this much more important, subjective side of our lives. And, if we can put even more attention on this all-important subjective side of our lives and truly discover how to grow from only 5-10% of our potential, into more of the 40-50% and then finally 70-100% of our latent potential, we will then find that all of the previous problems of humanity that have plagued us for so very long, now are completely gone and will have disappeared.

A weak man walking along the road encounters a big branch in front of him and it is a huge, impossible impediment to his progress and advancement. A strong man however, encounters this very tree and for him it is a morning exercise to pick that tree up and completely remove it from his path.

The sooner we all begin to tap and to discover 'how' we can most profoundly self-improve and dramatically self, un-fold we will then discover that universal formula for human success that will make our time and lives here upon this earth, that much more interesting and fulfilling.

CHAPTER 1

THE SCIENCE OF ASTROLOGY

"For all of our exalted technological progress,
civilization, is comparable to an axe in the hand of a
pathological criminal."

~ Albert Einstein

Previously in the past, we've long thought about the earth as
an intensely struggling and suffering place. Now, as we
discover more about this inherent subjective side of life; the
earth will be very soon, quite a different learning and growing
place!

Today, the entire field of astrology is becoming more accurate,
profound and perfect. And as these most extraordinary of
changes become more and more available for a wider and
wider portion of humanity, we will then see such a surprising
and most extraordinary true science of astrology, manifesting.

As a result of these many modern day astrological changes and
improvements we are now seeing the beginning of a more
coherent and well-integrated, reality of science becoming a
much more possibility for us, now.

In all of the ways that we recognize how any philosophy or
body of information needs to become 'scientific' so will now,
finally astrology be able to become a true science of life.

What had help back astrology from the past was the fact, that previously so much of astrology was disintegrated and not coherent or unified into one, wholeness of astrology. And those in the west especially who tried to study western astrology, they met with very meager results, just because that system had been so out of tune with the actual astronomy of the universe from above, which made such astrology in complete and much less effective.

That traditional eastern system also had its challenges and that hugely, fatalistic perspective has not been very modern or scientific because science believes that life is supposed to be improving and consistently more and more evolutionary.

The complete history of modern day science itself is a great testament as to how such knowledge and wisdom of life can be steadily and most profoundly improving every year, especially over these last 300 years that "science" has been such a part of human life, here upon our planet.

However, even this great tradition of scientific knowledge has encountered one huge obstacle along its path. Perhaps you've already heard of that physics discovering in the early part of this century which is called: "Heisenberg's Uncertainty Principles."

This is the very real, scientific realization that one can't get ultimate knowledge about any such objects in the universe because when one gets to that very subtle, quantum mechanical level and tries to perceive those ultimate building blocks of these sub-atomic particles; what has been discovered however, is that, this very act of subjectively looking, dramatically distorts and therefore manipulates ones attempt to find such ultimate knowledge and wisdom as to these subtlest of sub-atomic atoms or photons of light.

Even today, many decades later, this hugest of impediment

Within objective science, has not been resolved or solved. And no one within science seems capable of discovering how to resolve this deepest of modern day science quagmires because as it turns out, the final key to such ultimate knowledge, is NOT to be found in that same, objective field.

We have to go to that subjective side of us, that very part of us that is even now, doing that 'looking' and becoming more steady and stable, more mature and more enlightened within this subjective side of ourselves; then finally we will find ourselves in that very subjective-possibility who's very looking will not subvert or distort that perceptions of this relative universe.

Both of these two great, modern day revolutions going on within this all-important subjective side of ourselves will now finally give us that very special subjective wisdom to finally become ultimately aware as to truly, what life is all about.

And we can say, just how this modern day field of astrology is in fact becoming much more truly scientific today.

Take any idea, any human supposition, any concept or theory and what science proposes is that we develop a very important series of "experiments" which will allow anyone to test those very same theories and verify and validate these ideas or suppositions.

This is particularly possible now, because as one innocently explores one's own, particularly eastern chart, one will come to discover for one's very self, that one has been living this very real and most important of human, astrological natures.

With this natural scientific verification within one's self, one then can venture out and just as scientifically investigate as to how these same astrological ideas might also fit other people.

When I first began this slightly more outer, research, I first started with my family members and friends just because I sensed that I already more deeply knew them. And, as it turned out, it was a lot easier discovering 'how' their personal charts fit them just as profoundly which then catapulted me into beginning to study other individuals.

When I then branched out into my acquaintances and then strangers and got up to about 500 people, profoundly fitting their personal charts as well; I found myself rising up to such a greater, scientific appreciation that I would have ever thought possible.

Later when that number increased to 1,000 people and then, 2, 3 and even 4,000 people, all fitting their eastern charts, just as profoundly, I finally 'knew' that this astrology was in fact, so very real, and easily scientifically provable.

Though the chief stumbling block in such scientific astrological research from the past is how such unlearned, astrological individuals have attempted to study astrology outside and not within themselves. Because until you learn how to study that inherent personal astrological nature that you already are, you will not be able to so profoundly fathom how every other person too is living that unique astrology which is there very birth-life.

This situation also reminds me of something that I read from Einstein. He used to say: "I never feel that I have to be able to explain my ideas and theories to non-mathematicians. Because only the mathematically trained have the adequate skill and background in which to understand my new ideas of physics and relativity."

I think now this is very much like astrology. I now I can't really convince anyone else, 'intellectually' that astrology itself is so very real and important. I can however have a very deep and profound kind of conversation with other such astrologers who've also developed that unique perspective and training that is necessary to then understand astrology.

Though, there is one facet of astrology however, that makes this present situation much more significant. I now that I can in addition, help anyone to discover how their own, personal astrology does fit them as well. And, even within a few hours of personal astrological readings I can help anyone to more deeply appreciate the unique astrological nature that they always had been living but never quite understanding until now!

What mathematician could then be able to help any such mathematical novice wake up to these natural profundities of mathematics so very quickly and painlessly?

There is too one other unique facet of this astrology which will also have the most scientifically convincing and satisfying affects in terms of trying to verify and validate astrology.

This is that very unique and equally as important aspect of astrology which is called these "Transits" or daily horoscopes as they have been called in western astrology.

When I first began studying these more eastern mathematically derived Transits in 1989, I'd already learned how my own, personal eastern chart, already most profoundly fit me. However, when I then began watching these Transits of each day I then had the greatest astrological experience of my complete life.

I began to very directly experience for myself, how these very same astrological charts, which can so deeply and convincingly help one to better understand such human beings; these very same astrological charts can also be utilized to try and figure out what each day will be like! And after I first experienced that such an innocent astrological perspective could be so very revealing as to exactly 'why' each day, felt the unique ways that they did, I then had fairly soon, one of the greatest of all astrological revelations!

After about just three months, of watching each and every day, I realized: "Oh, my God, the universe itself is flowing within this very same, mathematics of this eastern astrology!"

This then was the most convincing and scientific proofs as to this reality of astrology than I ever thought would be possible. Though, I wondered too why this was so very surprising since I'd already discovered just how much 'my' and other people's charts also fit them.

Then, I realized this was particularly revealing because this now convinced me that this very nature and reality of astrology is not anything man-made. Instead it is in the very nature of life itself. Just as these atoms and sub-atomic particles are also so very real and such an intimate part of life itself.

So, is it that these astrological particles or quanta as we could describe them, are also in the very nature of life itself and existing both within human beings equally as within every moment of the creation and universe as it is in fact, flowing to us, each and every day.

As it turns out we are all in fact such unique "Astrological Beings" living in such a unique "Astrological Universe" and the sooner we discover this for ourselves, the sooner we'll really get what life is really, all about!

CHAPTER 2

THE SCIENCE OF CONSCIOUSNESS

"Human beings have an infinite potential within themselves.
And, now due to this simple technique of Transcendental
Meditation, everyone can unfold the full value of
consciousness within themselves."

~ His Holiness Maharishi Mahesh

We can also talk about that equally as important 'other' facet of our human natures and natural human-subjectivity which is our very unique consciousness, inner reality.

This field too is extremely old and ancient from the past, though, today too there have been such equally as important consciousness breakthroughs going on within this field which are also thrusting this unique subjective field into becoming such a true science of consciousness, as well.

For example, that one, unique Transcendental Meditation technique is that one, essential breakthrough which is already, most profoundly changing this entire, ancient, subjective field.

What is the most special and unusual about this single technique is the fact that this is the very first mediation procedure in hundreds and thousands of years, that finally understands that consciousness, self-development 'can' be completely easy and effortless to practice! This prospect then has not only made it possible for millions of people to now begin dramatically enlivening and expanding their very consciousnesses. But, as a result of this, such a huge body of research subjects now has made the study and investigation of consciousness so very easy to study, scientifically. Also, the fact that the head guru or founder of the T.M. movement was so very open and receptive to scientific research, today, more than 600 scientific studies have been done on such Transcendental meditators and all of those most amazing benefits and advantages that will come from such innocently meditating and expanding one's consciousness.

Because there has long been quite a bit of scientific research already conducted in terms of human physiology and EEG states of the mind, we have even today, such an exciting and profoundly insightful way of even more objectively understanding these subjective states of consciousness.

The 3 Typical Waking, Dreaming & Sleep States

Before meditation became so very much more popular in these last fifty years, for example, there was still quite a bit of information and even scientific interest in these primary, basic, three states of human existence. Every single human being, every day in fact, goes through each of these three main states of consciousness. We all find ourselves being awake at times and then we will end up sleeping and then dreaming.

What is particularly fascinating about this however, from a purely more scientific perspective is how each of these mental, threes states of subjective consciousness reality have already been correlated with such unique styles of physiological functioning including nervous system tests and EEG Brain tests as well.

One can even, hook up anyone in one room and measure their breath rate and brain wave patterns and string those wires into another room and completely 'see' when that person would then end up falling asleep and then dreaming, just by watching these changes in their physiological outputs and brain wave changes. One doesn't even to watch the person physically. One can simply watch those physiological changes and see when they are awake and when they dream and then when they deeply fall asleep.

Quite a bit of this initial research on meditating then has been in terms of these very same, physiological and mental Brain wave changes. It has not been deeply confirmed that "meditating" itself does indeed represent an unprecedented and most surprising, major 4th state of human consciousness which is as very real and scientifically verifiable as these previous 3 states of consciousness.

Such, present and future scientific research is continuing and is now researching and documenting these so-called Higher States of consciousness which expands this reality of human states of consciousness to 7 major states of consciousness.

As all of these continue to unfold and more and more is discovered about this most exciting and previously, most difficult field to study, even this most abstract aspect of our human natures, our very consciousnesses will become more completely understood and such a rather fulfilling and satisfying, true science of consciousness will then become such a more innocent and natural part of our life here upon this earth. And because it is said in most such consciousness and yoga philosophies that the human mind in " enlightenment" is a very settled and at peace mind while the typical, unenlightened human mind is anything but settled; therefore that human, monkey mind needs to be trained to prepare the mind to "transcend".

Transcendence is also said to be the very key to such development of the mind and this expansion of consciousness which can then help lead us to something as profound and monumental as our enlightenment!

The founder of this new and unique, Transcendental

Meditation technique believes that something has been missing in the long history and annals of yoga and consciousness philosophies.

This has been what he now calls the: "Natural Tendency" of the human mind. For the Maharishi, yes the mind is constantly moving. Yet inside that seemingly random, monkey mind jumping about, there is however a real reason for the mind's movements. For the Maharishi, there is an underlying reason why the human mind is constantly moving and as a result, unsettled and unenlightened.

The mind is moving but inside the human mind, there is this natural tendency of the mind which is to always be searching for greater and greater experiences of happiness. For the Maharishi, than, because the greater depths of the human mind are closer and closer to that field of pure consciousness which is the literal source of all thought; that reality of pure awareness would be a direct experience of limitless joy.

The #1 key than to meditating, effortlessly, would be if the human mind could be found moving in that direction of increasing joy and happiness from within. Therefore such meditating experiences could become completely easy and effortless just because that very nature of the human mind "is" already there to seek out such increasingly satisfying and fulfilling experiences.

What one learns to do, during this unique process of this special T.M. technique is 'how' to as if disengage oneself the typical, conscious, associative level of the mind and because that very nature of the human mind is to spontaneously move toward any such experiences which are in fact, more enjoyable and blissful, as a result, this most wonderful and significant of transcending experiences can be completely easy and effortless.

Today, some sixty-five years later after this unique T.M. experience has now been introduced into the world; now millions of individual have learned this very special technique and are experiencing this essential reality of consciousness itself. And, because this nature and reality of pure awareness is one of the most important of all life-realities, this greater scientific appreciation of this so very vital aspect of life, will end up being one of the most important of all, scientific insights. Consciousness itself is the very nature of life-itself. Inside this eternal churnings of the universe of stars, planets and galaxies, is that very nature of 'awareness' or consciousness which is the essential nature of all of life.

But because this inherent reality is so very abstract, it tends to be the most difficult area of life to figure out or understand. Now, however that this completely easy and effortless technique of Transcendental Meditation is now so readily available and is being studied so clearly, scientifically even; we can now talk about just what such a true science of consciousness could be all about.

The chief ways in which such a science of consciousness can continue to manifest in our world will be to:

#1 – Have any such individuals in the world, verify for themselves hat consciousness is such a real and most profound, human possibility.

#2 – Continue to increase the all-important scientific research that has been going on now for over 40 years.

#3 – And finally, when this natural Science of Consciousness is most profoundly united with all of the other, modern day sciences – then this wisdom of our latent, human potential will become an irresistible force for our entire world, culture!

CHAPTER 3

THE SCIENCE OF HUMAN SUBJECTIVITY!

"I think I am, therefore, I am….

I think….."

~ George Carlin

Though this entire field of human subjectivity has been the most difficult and hard for humanity to understand for hundreds and even thousands of years; today more is finally becoming well-understood about human subjectivity than ever before!

This is so very fortunate and vital because we are already so much more competent within the essential field of objective life.

We can now easily "put a Man on the Moon", create the most wondrous and powerful of computers, cars and smart-phones, but still, we have just as many human, subjective problems as ever before!

We have so many human problems, difficulties and frustrations which makes it even that much more important that we now discover how we can complement this outer, materialistic life with just such a deeper appreciation of this subjective side of life.

As it turns out there have always been these two, natural aspects of "subjective life" which have been our very consciousness and astrological natures. Every single human being gets born with one such, all-important consciousness, human nature. In other words we are all born conscious and aware. And it is this this very awareness that we have which sets us uniquely apart from the animals and grossest of physical realties which we call the rocks, trees and physical universe

But, because it has been so very hard to come to understand more clearly, this incessant consciousness that we have been, most of humanity has remained asleep as to that vast, potential of human life which can be unfolded as we learn how to unfold and expand our very consciousnesses!

Though, this field of consciousness has been around for hundreds and even thousands of years and there have been such "enlightened" individuals before who were able to talk about such an exquisite, inner reality.

For most of humanity, however, these human possibilities only remained as fanciful ideas and reflections of our imagination instead of being the very rock of our existence which it really, is!

Now, however, that this new and unique, easy and effortless technique of Transcendental Meditation has been re-discovered, we can finally talk about such a unique, science of consciousness which we can now take as readily advantage of as all of the other sciences of life.

Then there is too, that equally as important other facet of our human subjectivity which is our inherent "astrological natures".

As it turns out, every single human being, being born upon this earth, is one such just as important astrological personality and when enough people finally realize this for themselves, than astrology will become just as understood in terms of being such an intimate part of our human subjective natures.

With both of these two most recent breakthroughs in both of

These two aspects of consciousness and astrology, we now can finally begin formulating just what such a complete science of human subjectivity could be, all about!

Because both of these two most important aspects of our human natures, have been so poorly understood, **only more** of that inherently outer and more materialistic aspects of life were so well understood.

And, when only more of the outer and materialistic fields of life have predominated, than all kinds of almost innumerable, human subjectivity problems and difficulties have remained.

When we than learn how to combine both of these two, especially complete subjectivity fields of consciousness and astrology together, we will then have finally, such a complete and most well-understand "science of human subjectivity"!

This is particularly important because in the past, those that were interested in consciousness and expanding the human mind and achieving enlightenment, were not however also interested in astrology.

And, those on the other hand, who were so interested in astrology, were not found to be so interested or experts in this just as important field of consciousness.

We have been today, however, so very blessed because this most enlightened of individuals, His Holiness Maharishi Mahesh Yogi was one such individual whose personal enlightenment included both consciousness and astrology together.

When he lectured and taught he could just as easily talk about the great complexities and subtleties of astrology as well as consciousness itself.

Though he primarily talked about consciousness and that

inherent, vast human potential that exists within us all. He also, just as readily talked about his vision of enlightened astrology which as it turns out represented such a greater, most complete science of human SUBJECTIVITY!

Without such a natural appreciation of both the nature of consciousness and astrology, human life remained asleep as to this all-important subjective aspects of human life.

It is of course so very gratifying today, to see how both of these natural aspects of our subjective side are now, finally becoming so much more readily understood, today. And as these two greatest sciences of human subjectivity continue to become even much more well-understood, very soon, much of the negative repercussions of such an overly materialistic world, will finally be eliminated!

In fact we will judge our success just by seeing just how much human miseries, disappointments and human frustrations continue. And, we'll just as vividly be able to chart, our new success in this all-important subjective field by just how much of our previous subjective miseries are now longer dominating our lives and messing up our attempts to create such natural success and happiness, within our very lives.

When both of these two greatest of human discoveries continues to become even more well-known by hundreds of millions of individuals – then this greatest of all human-discovery will have the most surprising and extraordinary benefits for our entire culture.

It now rests with YOU!

If you find such a greatest of human discoveries within your own, very self – than this will be the greatest confirmation that such a reality is now indeed possible, for you

———

264

Our Guiding Light - His - Holiness
Maharishi Mahesh Yogi

"The Nature of Life Is Bliss."
"Knowledge is Structured In Consciousness."
"Knowledge Is The Greatest Purifier."
"Jyotish is the Eye of the Ved."

- Maharishi Mahesh Yogi

I am the most beholden to the unique genius and enlightenment of this one man, His Holiness Maharishi Mahesh Yogi who was one of the most enlightened of individuals to bless our earth in hundreds and even thousands of years!

His very special enlightenment gave him the ability to bring out this essential, greater knowledge and wisdom of this consciousness field and that uniqueness of that very special and specific technique of Transcendental Meditation has already completely revolutionized this complete field of consciousness today.

He was also so instrumental in helping science study such unique consciousness practices and encouraged scientists from all over the world, to both study and then bring out this rather new and yet, importantly profound knowledge and wisdom of this full range of consciousness. I am also the most appreciative to the Maharishi too, because it was from him too, who first brought out this highest possibility of astrology being capable and competent to help us achieve something the most profound as our enlightenment, in this life. From the very moment that he even began discussing how astrology could be both understood and practiced as one such enlightenment tool, I then much more deeply understood how astrology is supposed to be used as the most important of self-development tools!

This will be in retrospect one of the greatest of all human insights, because for hundreds and even thousands of years, astrology has only been well-known and practiced as one such "diagnostic" of tools. This means it has only been known as one such descriptive tool or 'why' we are the unique ways that we are. But from this very unique moment in 1987 when he first started describing astrology in such special enlightenment ways, then suddenly more began to be understood about astrology in terms of its self-development possibilities, than ever before.

He was the quintessential most enlightened individual but uniquely capable of bringing out that much needed, new knowledge and wisdoms, which have been so very necessary in our human civilization for hundreds and even thousands of years.

His one insight into meditation itself for example has already, vastly improved the entire field of meditation and consciousness expansion.

Already today, millions of people who would have probably never taken advantage of meditation before, have found it both inspiring and practical to now integrate such typically mysterious practices as meditation within their practical lives.

His one particularly most important insight that meditation itself could be completely easy and effortless to practice, is already vastly changing this entire field of historical consciousness and for the first time in recorded history, it is now being understood that the complete unfoldment of one's subjective, consciousness nature, can also be so very easy and effortless to unfold.

His unique insights into astrology will also in the very near future become valued and appreciated more deeply than ever before.

His very one particular revelation that astrology is meant to be used in such an important and vital of self-improvement ways will in the future, become more well-understood as the most profound of astrological insights in over 2,000 years!

Because from such a clearer and most profound self-improvement perspectives, astrology finally makes sense.

Previously almost all of astrology has been only that diagnostic oriented. It always sought to try and explain 'why' we all have been born with the unique human personalities and unique, human strengths and weaknesses that we each got born with.

But, nowhere in all of the recorded past of astrology has this unique insight and appreciation of the self-transformative nature and potential of astrology been so well-understood or even written about.

As a result the real power and significance of astrology has long been lacking and as a result, the all-important nature and condition of humanity has not much improved over hundreds and even thousands of years.

That's why we continue to see such human difficulties as greed, selfishness, egocentric battles and emotional and mental problems continuing to dominate and exist in our human society in spite of the fact that we can put such "men" on the Moon.

Why even the other day I was reading about how one special billionaire in the world wants to help send a million people to Mars as soon as possible. I, of course find it so very deeply frustrating to contemplate such outer expansion possibilities because the very interior essence of most individuals in the world today, is still so very poor and undeveloped.

However, with just this innocent addition of this "new" astrology coming into the world today, we now have that unique knowledge and wisdom which will allow anyone to discover 'who' they are and most importantly, 'whom' they're meant to self-evolve into! When astrology becomes more well-understood in this all-important and crucial of ways than the very quality of human life upon our earth, will finally improve!

AUTHOR – MARK KINCAID

"If God can work through me, he can work through anyone."

~ Saint Assisi

Author: Born on one such September 4th of 1951.

Looking back over my entire adult life I can clearly see that if I had not learned how to meditate, (in 1971) and how to then understand how astrology could be used in one such important of self-development ways, (1987), my own, interior, personal life would have not become nearly as positive or fulfilling as it has become.

I would have instead continued being shy, self-conscious and full of so many pervasive and frustrating, emotional and mental problems in my life. I can easily compare my life to some of my friends in high school and especially in terms of those who never learned how to meditate, I see that their lives did not become nearly as happy or glorious as mine.

I am of course, the most grateful and appreciative to the Maharishi for him making the individual choice to bring out his unique enlightenments into the world, which we have now been blessed with for over much of the last 50 years.

I can't even imagine how different our world would have been if this supreme value of consciousness had not become such an intimate part of our world experience in this last half of century, now. I first learned how to meditate in 1971 which right away, profoundly changed my life.

Then later to be guided to such a new and unprecedented "astrology for enlightenment" by that same great, Maharishi –

now I see how both of these greatest of Maharishi revelations are the key two elements to this Greatest Human Discovery of all time.

I was never anything special from my humble beginnings upon this earth. Though, if I have to point to any positive part of my inner life – it was that I knew I had much great self-need. And this one aspect to my life, this greater receptivity – drew to me, such greater teachers and gurus and I gained as much wisdom from my many astrology teachers as the Maharishi, himself.

Though it took me personally, decades to find just how to both understand and integrate these two greatest of subject fields of consciousness and astrology, together. Now, I now however, just how much more easy it is for such present day students who are gaining the greatest advantage of these two breakthroughs being more clearly 'seen' now.

Though I am looking forward soon, to look down from my astral heaven, after this earth, to then see how much our world will soon be benefiting from this greatest of all human discoveries, which of course every new generation will need to unfold for themselves. Jai Guru Dev......